A CONCISE

COLLEGE SUCCESS

John Arthur

BINGHAMTON UNIVERSITY
STATE UNIVERSITY OF NEW YORK

PEARSON

Prentice
Hall

Upper Saddle River, New Jersey
Columbus, Ohio

Library of Congress Cataloging-in-Publication Data

Arthur, John.
    A concise guide to college success : carpe diem / John Arthur.
       p. cm.
    Includes bibliographical references and index.
    ISBN 0-13-112934-1
    1. College student orientation.   2. Study skills.   3. Academic writing.   I. Title: Carpe diem.
  II. Title.

LB2343.3.A78 2004
378.1'0281—dc21

2003053553

Vice President and Executive Publisher: Jeffery W. Johnston
Senior Acquisitions Editor: Sande Johnson
Assistant Editor: Cecilia Johnson
Editorial Assistant: Erin Anderson
Production Editor: Holcomb Hathaway
Design Coordinator: Diane C. Lorenzo
Cover Designer: Jeff Vanik
Cover Image: Corbis
Production Manager: Pamela D. Bennett
Director of Marketing: Ann Castel Davis
Director of Advertising: Kevin Flanagan
Marketing Manager: Christina Quadhamer
Compositor: Aerocraft Charter Art Service
Cover Printer: The Lehigh Press, Inc.
Printer/Binder: R. R. Donnelley & Sons Company

Pearson Education Ltd.
Pearson Education Singapore Pte. Ltd.
Pearson Education Canada, Ltd.
Pearson Education–Japan

Pearson Education Australia Pty. Limited
Pearson Education North Asia Ltd.
Pearson Educación de Mexico, S.A. de C.V.
Pearson Education Malaysia Pte. Ltd.

10 9 8 7 6 5 4 3 2 1
ISBN 0-13-112934-1

brief contents

contents

HOW TO SUCCEED IN THE CLASSROOM   15

THE CARE AND FEEDING OF PROFESSORS   29

LOGIC AND CRITICAL THINKING
TOOLS OF THE TRADE   37

HOW TO READ
AND UNDERSTAND WHAT YOU ARE READING   69

HOW TO DO WELL ON EXAMS   77

HOW TO WRITE A GOOD PAPER   81

PART TWO

The Rules of the Road   99

CHEATING AND ACADEMIC HONESTY   101

LANGUAGE USE   105

10 GRAMMAR   121

11 PUNCTUATION   127

preface to students

a student's job isn't easy. I remember it as exciting and challenging, but also stressful. It's tough being constantly evaluated, week in and week out. That's the bad news. The good news is that it's almost certainly a once-in-a-lifetime experience: rarely do people get graded and tested so much. The other piece of good news is that if you can manage the stress, being a student can be the most exciting and enriching period in your life. You can then "seize the day"—*carpe diem*.

I wrote this book for two simple reasons: (1) to help students like you get as much as possible from your college education and (2) to help you excel in the courses you take. I assume that students want to do better in classes. Sometimes you may be motivated by the desire to get into a good graduate, medical, or law school—a perfectly reasonable goal. Or maybe you have other reasons (I suggest some others in the first chapter). Whatever your reasons, I wrote *A Concise Guide to College Success* to help you succeed in college, do better in classes, and improve your reading and writing skills. I also hope to make you see the value—and the fun—of learning and of education in general. But more on that in a moment.

As long as we're doing introductions, I should say something here about myself. I graduated from Cornell College and went on to graduate school at Vanderbilt University, where I got a Ph.D. in Philosophy and then an M.A. in Political Sociology. (No, I never burned a flag to protest the Vietnam War, though I did *wash* one in 1969. But that's another story.) I also spent two years at Harvard Law School, where I became even more convinced that being a professor was the right thing for me after all, even though I'd always assumed I would be a lawyer. I did, however, meet my wife, Amy, at Harvard, so it was worth it for that reason alone. Amy *is* a lawyer, and also a critic— as you'll see. Our most recent travels took us to Oxford, where I spent a year as a Visiting Fellow at Balliol College and she studied law.

As for publishing, besides a variety of articles and two books on political and philosophical topics, *The Unfinished Constitution* (1989) and *Words That Bind* (1995), I've also edited or co-edited seven books. These include *Morality and Moral Controversies* (sixth edition, 2002), *Readings in Philosophy of Law* (third edition, 1998), *Justice and Economic Distribution* (second edition, 1991), and *Color – Class – Identity: The New Politics of Race* (1996). I've taught philosophy for more than 20 years at a variety of colleges and universities, including Brandeis, the College of Charleston, Harvard, Lake Forest College, Tennessee State University, the State University of New York at Binghamton, and (in England) the University of East Anglia. So the odds are at some point I've taught at a college or university like yours. I've also been chair of two departments and am now director of the Program in Philosophy, Politics, and Law at the State University of New York at Binghamton. We have 300 majors in our program, most of whom go on to law school. So I guess I've never really escaped law after all, now that I think about it.

My main teaching interests are law and politics. In the classroom, I'm best known for calling on students in the style of law schools, even in a large lecture course of more than 200 (actually, I don't really "lecture" much at all). I'm proud to say that I've won two awards for my teaching.

As you can perhaps already tell, this book is written in a direct, informal style. That was intentional, though it is not the style you should use in formal academic writing, such as exams and papers. It is the right style here, however.

Many people contributed to this book in lots of different ways. An original inspiration came from a conversation many years ago with a friend and teacher, Jeri Perlmutter, who explained to me some interesting research on teaching and learning. Some of her ideas found their way into this book. I also want to thank especially Steve Scalet, David Strauss, Elliot Leffler, Rebecca Haimowitz, Sarah Leffler, Tim O'Hagan, Marc Shapiro, and Bill Throop for their helpful suggestions. Most important, my aforementioned wife, Amy Shapiro, read and commented on the manuscript with much care and patience.

John Arthur

preface to instructors

ORIGINS OF THIS BOOK

*t*he aim of this book is to enable students, working alone or with the help of faculty members, to acquire the basic tools necessary to succeed in college. No book can do that by itself, of course. It requires the work of talented, committed instructors as well as of students themselves.

This book began life as handouts I prepared for distribution to my own classes, which I would sometimes supplement with a short book on grammar, punctuation, and other aspects of writing. But as time went by, I became unhappy with that approach. Most of the supplementary books were long and expensive, so I found myself adding more to the handouts I was providing. I wanted material that is brief and to the point and that addresses students at all levels in an honest, straightforward manner that could help them with the myriad problems they face while studying, taking examinations, and writing papers. I also wanted material students could use to improve their reasoning skills as well as their grammar, punctuation, and other areas where they sometimes have problems. Encouraged by the reactions of my students and other faculty who have used the material themselves, I revised the material and added sections on time management and study habits, reading skills, note taking, learning styles, getting along with professors, academic honesty, and much more. What you have in your hands is the result of that process.

As a philosopher, I also could not resist the temptation to introduce some philosophical issues and ideas as they became relevant. So, for instance, there is a brief discussion of the nature of a successful life and its relationship to financial success and to happiness. I then discuss the role of education in a happy, successful life, the nature and moral importance of such virtues as diligence and open-mindedness, and the educational significance of intellectual and cultural diversity. There are even brief discussions of the nature of reason, free speech, and the important role of the university.

Thus the book is quite ambitious. Besides giving solid, practical advice to students on topics ranging from time management and study skills to choosing a major and getting along with professors, I also discuss larger issues involving values. These include reasons for being in college, which led me in turn to consider questions about how we are to judge a life happy and successful. I also give both students and the instructors who work with them some brief "Rules of the Road," including the basics of grammar, punctuation, language use, and writing. Finally, I tried to make it all easy and fun to read.

I've benefited greatly over the many years that I have used this material in my classes, and as I prepared this book, from valuable suggestions by students, reviewers, and instructors who have used the material in their own courses. (I mention many of these students and colleagues at the end of the Preface to Students.) In that sense, it is very much a group project.

USES OF THIS BOOK

*b*ecause of its breadth and brevity, the book can be used many ways by instructors working in a variety of contexts. Some instructors could use it as part of an orientation program for new students at their university, either before classes begin or during the first few weeks of the semester. Others, like me, could use it in specific courses, assigning parts of it as they become relevant and using the sections on logic and critical thinking, language, grammar, and punctuation.

I have tried hard to make the book as flexible as possible. The chapters have no particular order, so instructors can assign them however they think best. Since they are freestanding, it is always possible to skip any particular one. While some instructors may choose to go through the book chapter by chapter, discussing the ideas presented and going over the exercises and problems, others may ask students just to read some or even all of the chapters on their own. Still others may want to use specific chapters to work with students in more detail, perhaps as they prepare to write papers or take exams. Because the sections are brief, students can easily learn the basics of how to use a semicolon and comma, where to put punctuation marks, why active voice is generally better than passive, and how to avoid verbosity and wordiness (as well as understand what those are). Instructors all have their own time-tested approaches.

At the suggestion of reviewers, I have provided questions and exercises for each of the chapters in Part One. These vary widely, depending on the topic of the chapter and the goal of the exercises. Sometimes I ask students simply to explain ideas that are in the text. Other times I provide exercises that test students' ability to use the skills they have learned, for example, in logic and critical thinking. Often, though, the exercises do not have a uniquely correct answer because they ask students to think about their own values, observe their study habits, assess their goals in college, or reflect critically on what has been said in the text. I have, however, provided brief answers to Chapter 4's logic and critical thinking exercises in an appendix.

A WORD ABOUT THE APPROACH

Sometimes professors take the attitude that it's not their job to teach students to study, to improve students' writing, or even to teach the rules of grammar and punctuation. Students should have learned those skills in high school, it is said, and these professors' responsibilities are limited to providing good lectures and lively discussions on the course material. I know this view well and have defended it myself at times. But I have since changed my mind, and I think it is important to take students where I find them: if they are not ready to write a well-organized essay with correct grammar and punctuation, I no longer feel comfortable thinking that it is their (or the English department's) problem alone. Indeed, I have found it tremendously rewarding helping students with writing. Some students appreciate it more than anything else I do for them.

I have also found that a no-nonsense, direct approach works much better than a more passive, vague one. Rather than the teachers who accepted poor work, the teachers who taught me to write were the ones with high standards—often higher than I could hope to meet—who sometimes covered my papers with red ink. One of my own students recently recalled, fondly, how her favorite high school teacher had actually made her cry with his critical comments. From him, she reported, she had finally learned to write. Of course, I am not advocating being harsh, let alone cruel—far from it! But I do think it is important to be honest, to let students know if they have problems, and to work on those problems. As I emphasize in this book, *great* writing is rare, but in my experience, almost any student can be brought to the level of a decent writer. And decent writing that is clear and part of a well-organized essay is almost always perfectly adequate to the task.

In recent years, I have discovered a somewhat unusual but successful method of teaching writing that puts this book to good use. I ask students to write a series of short, 1,000-word essays. Sometimes it is to be nothing more than a synopsis of the day's reading; other times it is more critical and personal. Students are required to earn at least a certain number of points (perhaps 16) during the semester with their writing. Each essay, I tell them, is worth up to 4 points, so in theory they could meet this requirement with only four assignments. Soon it becomes apparent which students need help, since they earn only 1 or 2 points on their first essays. I have everybody whose writing needs serious work meet with me. I then go over their essay (or at least a decent part of it) with them line by line, asking them, when necessary, to explain what a sentence means, and showing them how to improve punctuation, word choice, spelling, and organization. I have found various chapters of this book useful in this process. For students who are already adequate writers but who have a specific problem, I simply refer them to the relevant sections in the book (on semicolons or commas, for instance, or perhaps on correct citation form). In that way, *A Concise Guide to College Success* becomes a common reference book for the entire class.

Finally, let me add that I would love to hear from you or your students about this book, including suggested revisions, additional topics, and exercises. I can be reached via email at jarthur@binghamton.edu.

ACKNOWLEDGMENTS

*m*y sincere thanks to the following individuals, who reviewed this text and offered constructive suggestions for its improvement: Betty Fortune, Houston Community College; M. Debnam Chappell, Fairfield University; M. Endrinal, Houston Community College; Dawn Graziani, Santa Fe Community College; Cheryl Rice, State University of West Georgia; and Janette Thomas, Alfred State College.

My thanks, too, to Anna Feigenbaum, author of *Grammar and Other Diseases,* who contributed her poem to this book.

PART ONE

Getting the Most Out of College

the value of an education

SUCCESS IN LIFE AND THE ROLE OF MONEY

Let's begin in what may seem an unusual place for a book like this and discuss what you can hope to get out of your years in college and the importance of money in a successful life. I'll start by asking what's the point of your being in college? One answer, and it is not a bad one, is that people who graduate from college earn more money—usually lots more. So if money matters to you, and especially if having a lot of it matters, then you have a reason to be where you are. But I want to suggest another, in some ways more important, reason for you to consider. Indeed, it may ultimately be the most important reason of all. We should begin by thinking about what matters in life, and why.

We all care, I assume, about whether or not our lives are successful. Because we are human rather than lower animals, the question is unavoidable. Even if we feel,

3

in the end, that we have mostly achieved our objectives or satisfied our most important wishes, the question still remains whether those objectives and desires were worth pursuing. Was what we valued really valuable? If the answer is "no," then our life was a failure. And to come to realize that one's life was wasted, spent in a way that is unworthy of a human life, is a fearsome prospect.

Just today I read an article in the *Wall Street Journal* in which stockbrokers were interviewed about the economy and the current state of their business. One of the more philosophical brokers made an observation that is relevant here. He said that he has noticed something interesting about his clients, some of whom are very wealthy and others who are not. The happiest ones, financially and otherwise, were professors (I am not making this up; in case you don't know, professors are not among the wealthy in this society). Yet why should that be? It was not, as you might expect, for any high-falutin' reason, such as that they get to think deep thoughts or even that they have summers off to do what they want. The reason, he said, is that—unlike his far richer clients—professors believe that they have enough money and that their lives are successful. I was also reminded of another study I saw recently in which people of different economic levels were asked how much money they thought they would need to be happy. What is interesting is that at almost *every* level of income, people said the same thing: to be financially satisfied, they need just slightly more—usually around 10 percent—than they currently earn.

There is a lesson here. The chance of having a successful, satisfying life depends on many things, including health, friendships, and financial security. Some of these are beyond our control and therefore are not my concern here. But many are within our control, including the role of money. Most people think that, for themselves at least, money is merely a means to an end rather than an end in itself. But many people who say they believe that actually don't. For them, their income and salaries are how they keep score, how they measure their success. Money is not a means to an end but has itself become the end. You can see this when raise time comes around. Often people are happy with their raises until they learn others got more. Other times a person may be unhappy, until it emerges that the person's raise was more than most. Why is that? Not, I take it, because they have suddenly decided they need, or don't need, that money for something else. It's because money is their measure of success. Higher earnings, relative to others, has become the goal.

The problem with using money as a scorecard is its effect on people's lives. That same stockbroker, when discussing the lives of his wealthier clients, described them as dominated by long airplane trips—with the stale air and bad food that go with them—and long hours spent at the office. All that means time not spent on other things, whether family and friends, hobbies, learning about the world, reading novels, following or participating in local politics, listening to or playing music, playing sports, or any number of other far more interesting and ultimately more rewarding activities. All of which raises the next question: What, precisely, is a successful life, by which I mean simply a life that is worthy of a person, and not one that was wasted and should be regretted? (What I have to say here is not meant to force you to believe something new and alien but instead to remind and make plain what we both, in a sense, already know.)

For us, a successful life has two components: enjoyable experiences and worthwhile accomplishments. Success includes having experiences that are enjoyable, in whatever form that may take. Pleasures are one type, of course, whether they be the experience of food, sex, relaxation, or whatever. But we also enjoy other experiences, such as being loved and respected, belonging to a group, and even engaging in physical or intellectual struggle and competition. By accomplishments I mean not how things feel from inside but the actual fact of doing what is worthwhile. Accomplishment includes a vast range of outcomes, but they all in some sense make the world a better place. Maybe they allow for less cruelty, injustice, ignorance, or suffering, or perhaps they create more worthwhile art, music, or literature. Creating and raising children whose lives are themselves valuable is an obvious mark of success. So, just as a life may be judged a failure for pursuing a worthless goal (counting the blades of grass in my lawn comes to mind), a life is made successful in part by having accomplished what was worth doing.

We should be open-minded about the right mix of these two. I don't want to say either that a life of great accomplishment but little enjoyment is a failure or that a life full of enjoyable experiences but few accomplishments is unsuccessful. Mother Teresa's life should be judged a success whether or not she had many enjoyable experiences, just as a connoisseur may be said to have had a successful life though he accomplished very little beyond his own enjoyment. The best, most successful life would probably include both enjoyment and accomplishment, but that does not mean either is necessary for a person to be able to say, truly, that life was a success.

Happiness raises a slightly different question from whether or not a life is successful, for happiness depends on the attitude we take toward our own life rather than whether it was successful. As I suggested, whether a life was a success is open to dispute; it's a matter of whether the life was relatively full of accomplishments or enjoyable experiences. To be *happy*, however, is to be pleased with one's life—to take an affirmative attitude toward it. That means, then, that a person can be happy even if her life was not successful, and may be unhappy even if the life was a genuine success from our perspective. Suppose Mother Teresa (whose life, I am supposing, was in fact a success) was herself deeply distressed that she had never created a great work of art, the only thing she thought could make for a successful life. While you and I might agree that she was wrong, and that despite her own feelings her life was in fact quite successful, if she believes that, then her life would have been in an important sense an unhappy one. Similarly, a person whose life was wasted or even was full of evil deeds might nonetheless still have been happy because that person believed that his life was full of worthwhile accomplishments. The lesson, then, is both that we want our lives to be successful and that to be happy we must also affirm our lives as a success.

THE PLACE OF EDUCATION IN A SUCCESSFUL LIFE

*i*f what I have said is right, then perhaps we can see now why so many wealthy people seem to be, and indeed are, unhappy with their lives: they see themselves as unsuccessful. Having lots of money guarantees neither enjoyment nor accomplishment and therefore cannot ensure a successful life. Those who realize this fact, sometimes too late, are unable to affirm their lives and are unhappy. Merely owning things, without the time and the knowledge to appreciate them, is in the end not a very satisfying experience. And so, unless the money is a means to accomplishing worthy ends (enjoyment and accomplishments) it will play no role in judging a life successful. It is a grave mistake to use it to keep score, as if merely acquiring money were itself a mark of success.

This is where education comes in. Whether formal or not, education is an important component of a successful life. But how, exactly, is education important to a life's success (now assuming that success can be measured in terms of enjoyment and accomplishment)?

My wife, Amy, loves to play the violin (and the fiddle), and owning a fine Stradivarius violin would be a great source of joy to her. But that's not because merely owning it, or having the money to buy it, is itself important. It isn't. It's because she knows and loves music so much that she can appreciate such an instrument. If she did not have her interest in music, owning the Stradivarius would give her little enjoyment.

My real point has nothing to do with Amy and her violins, however. It involves education. How is it that people are able to have enjoyable experiences? Sometimes, of course, it's biological and natural (such as food and sex). But these are only the beginning of the human capacity for enjoyment. In fact, we can learn to enjoy all kinds of things, and that, I suggest, is partly what education is about. Whether it's art, history, philosophy, religion, music, math, physics, sports, or whatever, college offers a great opportunity to develop interests and capacities that can put people—you—in a position to have a rich (in the best sense of that term) and enjoyable life. But merely owning things is rarely a source of real enjoyment or accomplishment, and acquiring large amounts of money rarely, by itself, produces a happy life. Don't get me wrong. I am not saying money is unimportant. My point, rather, is that its importance depends on whether we are able to use it to good ends, that is, to accomplish worthwhile goals or produce enjoyable experiences. By itself, it guarantees neither a successful nor a happy life.

Surprisingly, perhaps, Yale law professor Anthony Kronman discusses these same issues in his book on the changing legal profession, *The Lost Lawyer* (Harvard University Press, 1993). Recent studies have noted sharp declines in job satisfaction among lawyers (and also doctors), with some studies reporting that as many as half of all practicing lawyers regret having gone into the profession. Kronman argues that this attitude is the direct result of changes in the nature of legal practice. As lawyers have moved into larger law firms where they specialize more in particular areas of law, they have lost touch with anything but the narrowest concerns their clients may have. The older ideal was of a "lawyer statesman," whose concerns for a client extended beyond such instrumental ones as how to draw a will, avoid a lawsuit, or make a contract. Like medicine, legal practice used to demand of lawyers that they know their clients and be able to offer advice about whether a course of action was what they *should* want or was in their *genuine* interests. Now, however, legal practice is more like being a hired gun. It focuses on the immediate, specialized problem posed by a person the lawyer hardly knows or may never have met. That change matters very much, according to Kronman, because it means lawyers are no longer able to exercise what, following Aristotle, he terms "practical wisdom." Legal practice has become a less satisfying experience even as it has made its practitioners much wealthier. This has happened because the complex range of judgments necessary to give clients solid, impartial moral and practical advice is no longer needed or used, having been replaced by shallow, technical know-how. Kronman's conclusion is that law has become, and will remain, a less satisfying profession precisely because it no longer allows—let alone demands—that its practitioners exercise those capacities of judgment that are integral to a satisfying life. It no longer fosters, or requires, practical wisdom.

The lesson here is as simple as it is important, and it applies to medicine and other professions, to decisions you make in college, to choosing a career, and beyond. As we struggle to understand what experiences will contribute to making a successful life, it is important to pay attention to the nature of the activities we engage in and, in particular, to the quality of the experiences we expect to have. Kronman's specific suggestion is that people are most satisfied and happy when allowed (or required) to develop higher capacities of practical wisdom—which include moral reflection and impartiality—and then to employ those capacities in their professional lives. Developing talents and exercising capacities are integral to successful lives, and when law and other professions do not foster them, their practitioners are less satisfied and their lives less successful.

This is relevant in choosing a job because it is so tempting to suppose that income is the most important factor, overshadowing the ability to use our higher moral and other capacities to give advice to clients, to create something worthwhile, to develop leadership skills, to be artistically creative, and to learn about the natural world. So while college is not absolutely essential, by any means, to development of those higher capacities whose exercise is part of a successful life, it is, for many, a unique chance.

One final thought, in the form of an anecdote. Students who came to college with credits from high school or who have taken courses in summer school sometimes ask me, as their advisor, if I think they should try to graduate in three years or stay on and take "unnecessary" classes. Others ask me if I think it is good to take a year off after graduation before going to graduate or professional school. My answer is always the same. I ask them what they will do with that last year in college or while waiting to go on in school. Sometimes they describe a course or two they would like to take or reveal that they would like to go into the Peace Corps, teach, do an internship, travel, or work. Then I ask them to suppose they were on their deathbed looking back on their lives, and to think about whether they would then regret, at the very end of their life, having spent only 48 years at whatever career they plan to pursue rather than 49. Would they trade one more year on the job for that experience in college, the Peace Corps, or whatever? Most say they would not make the trade, and perhaps now it is clear why. They would have missed a valuable opportunity to use the fourth year in college to develop interests, talents, and capacities that would contribute far more to a successful, rich, and interesting life than any alternative. Not taking advantage of college wastes money, of course, but it also wastes a once-in-a-lifetime opportunity to think about what, for you, would be a successful life and to acquire the interests and develop the capacities necessary to achieve it.

LIFE OUTSIDE THE CLASSROOM: ACTIVITIES AND THE VALUE OF DIVERSITY

*i*n this section I offer a few thoughts about college life beyond the classroom. Though I am a professor and not a psychologist, these thoughts reflect my experience teaching thousands of students over many years at many different universities. It is very clear to me that success in college depends in part on what happens outside the classroom. Sometimes students get into trouble, of course; other times their outside experiences contribute in important ways to their success in college.

First, the possible problems. Drinking too much or taking other drugs really is a problem for many students. Getting arrested is only the most obvious cost. I have seen otherwise bright, hard-working students' careers and lives literally destroyed by excessive drinking or drug taking. If you feel you are having a problem in this or any other area, such as depression, don't hesitate to get help. Universities have counseling centers or other professionals who will help you. And you can always go to an advisor or trusted faculty member.

On a happier note, positive outside activities are important. Sensible people do not live their lives for grades any more than for money. Grades matter, of course. For one thing, they reflect to some degree how much a student got out of the class, which can also show how useful the course will be if applied later in life. Grades also are important when applying to graduate school or for a job. But there is much more to succeeding in college than getting good grades. Indeed, I think that participating in a variety of activities can be an important, and maybe even the *most important,* part of having a successful college experience. (When I was in college, I even joined a fraternity. It was an experience—I still have the paddle somewhere in the basement. Eventually, though, I decided that I wanted to do other things with my time, including political organizing, playing tennis, and courting a girlfriend, so I "depledged." But I never regretted that I had joined.)

Most universities and colleges have free lectures, concerts, and movies. These can be wonderful or awful. Don't be put off if you go to a lecture, for instance, and it's boring or worse. Sometimes it can be fun to watch how people, including perhaps your professors, react to a bad speaker. And when the lecture is over, at least you will have done something different, as opposed to yet another, indistinguishable couple hours spent watching television or whatever.

But lectures and concerts are only the tip of the iceberg. Most universities also have a wonderful variety of student-centered activities and groups you can join, including varsity and intramural sports, theater, music, and debate as well as preprofessional groups, social groups, religious groups, political groups of all stripes, and much more.

One well-documented problem, even at diverse institutions like my own, is that students tend to hang out with others who are like themselves. Many university-sponsored groups and activities offer a chance to meet people outside your own circle, many of whom may be from different religious, racial, and ethnic backgrounds. That can by itself be a valuable learning experience. Such groups and activities also provide a great opportunity to try out new sides of your personality, to develop new talents, and to learn to enjoy different kinds of experiences. You can discover more about yourself and develop interests that will enrich your life long after you leave college. All of this is very important, for how much you enjoy college, for the success you have in college, and for your life after you leave. Indeed, studies have shown that the best indicator for how satisfied students are with their college experience after they have graduated is how involved they were in activities outside the classroom, especially ones that involved topics discussed in the classroom.

CHOOSING CLASSES AND A MAJOR

Still, you face the question of which courses you should take and what major you should choose. These are important questions, though not as important as people sometimes think. As you may have gathered from my earlier remarks about the value of education, I think it's important to take a variety of courses in many different areas. That includes everything from music and art to math, history, and politics. (Did I mention philosophy?) There are many good reasons for this. First, you never know what might pique your interest until you try it. I never thought I'd like logic (it sounded very dry to me), but once I was in the class I loved it; the same goes for economics. Another reason for choosing a broad range of courses is that you never know where you will end up and what courses may prove useful. Calculus might seem irrelevant now, as might economics. But later on, if you go into business or to law school, they both may be very helpful. I'd also choose at least some difficult courses. I am not saying that grade point average is unimportant, but admissions committees and employers aren't stupid. They know that some courses, and areas, are much harder than others, so a person with a high GPA but easy classes is not necessarily better off than another who did less well but took much more difficult classes. Having taken more difficult classes also says something interesting about a person's character (for example, that she's not one to take the easy way out).

A final rule of thumb is to take teachers, not courses. Some of the classes I enjoyed the least, and in which I learned the least, sounded great on paper. On the other hand, often a course in an area where I had no interest turned out to be a favorite. The professor generated the interest. The logic course I mentioned was taught by a terrific professor, which had a lot to do with how much I enjoyed and learned in the course.

Another important question is whether to take hard or easy professors. My answer is "neither—take good teachers." By a good teacher, I mean one whose class you will find interesting and from whom you will learn. In general, students learn more from teachers who have higher expectations, that is, who give relatively low grades. But that is not always true. Some good teachers are relatively easy graders, and some pretty bad ones are hard. (I myself tend toward the hard side, judging from student evaluations. Amy says I'm a difficult grader because, unlike her, I didn't always work hard in college. I think I have better reasons though. You should take good teachers because they will teach you more; besides getting a degree, that's why you are in college.)

Students also sometimes wonder how important which major they choose is. In truth, it often matters less than many imagine. Here's how to think about it. On one hand, for example, if you know you intend to be a doctor or get a job in business, then you *should* seek advice from people in the know about such things. Unlike law, medical schools have a prescribed curriculum. Other programs do also, so it's important to get that bit of information early and to act accordingly. But many other students will not be limited by future career plans. Law schools accept virtually any major. For them, the important questions involve whether a person can write and think well.

It's also worth keeping in mind that most majors leave plenty of room for other courses, from all-college requirements to electives and even a minor or second major. So choosing a major is really nothing more than deciding that perhaps a third of your total college education will be in that area. Other courses matter a lot too, for the reasons I have already discussed. As for second majors and minors, my advice again is to follow your own interests and inclinations. But it *is* clear that merely having a second major is not, by itself, a sign that you accomplished more. What it really means is that you limited yourself by focusing on a second major rather than taking a broader variety of courses, something that is not necessarily easier or wiser. And again, graduate and professional school admissions committees know that, as do prospective employers. So I'd advise against second majors for their own sake, unless you have a special interest or want to emphasize your background in that area after graduation.

TWO KEY VIRTUES: DILIGENCE AND OPEN-MINDEDNESS

I once had a student who was a very good wrestler. I wrestled for a short time in college myself and can assure you it is one of the most, if not *the* most, demanding of all sports. My student and his team-mates used to run up and down the stairs of a 15-story building, over and over, *after* they were through with a grueling practice. I remember this student telling me, as he went off to a very competitive law school, that he was sure he would do well. He was not, he said, going to be the smartest student in his class, having barely made it off the waiting list. But one thing he said he knew for sure was that nobody in that law school was going to "outwork" him. Having been a wrestler, he knew very well how much hard work and self-discipline he was capable of. He did, in fact, do well.

To be honest, many students in college don't work terribly hard. What that means, then, is that even if, like my former student, you aren't one who learns material particularly easily, you can still do very well by simply putting forth more effort. Setting goals, sticking to them even if you fall down now and then, and working hard are very important.

Besides diligence, another trait that is vitally important for college success is to be open-minded. I do not mean that you tolerate everything and everybody. That's not open-mindedness—it's lack of standards. I mean the willingness not just to listen but to actually hear, whether it is other students, professors, or something you are reading. This is not as easy as it sounds because it requires coming to understand not just that people are different—we all know that—but that other people may have something to say that is valuable no matter how foreign or implausible it may sound initially.

Imagination is an important part of open-mindedness. Sometimes we don't appreciate what somebody else is saying because we haven't yet been able to imagine what people's experiences have been like, what they value and why, or where they come from culturally and religiously. Yet it is very difficult to learn without the ability to appreciate others' points of view and to imagine how the world looks from their perspectives.

Given the importance of diligence and open-mindedness, what can you do about it, especially if one or the other does not come naturally to you? While we can't change ourselves easily or overnight, people do have a lot of influence on their own character. When I discuss study habits and doing class work later, I will offer some specific suggestions about how to make it easier to be diligent and self-disciplined. But there's another important point to keep in mind besides those practical suggestions. We are all influenced by those around us. That means that if you hang around with lazy, narrow-minded students who think they have little to learn from people who are different from themselves, you will tend to develop those same traits. It also means, on the other hand, that if your friends study hard, are tolerant, and want to be open to new ideas, you will find it much easier to be that way yourself. Aristotle was the first person, as far as I know, to appreciate the profound importance of our friends for the development of our character. I think he was right.

Review Questions and Exercises

1. How does the author define a "successful" life? Do you agree or disagree? If you agree, explain what you think a critic might say is wrong about the definition and your response to the objection. If you disagree, explain why you disagree.

2. What is happiness, and how does it differ from success in life? What is the role of education in a successful life?

3. Do you agree that money is almost never, by itself, the basis of a successful life? Explain.

4. What are diligence and open-mindedness and why are they "key" virtues of students?

5. If you have chosen a major, write an essay in which you explain why you chose it and how that decision is related to your overall goals. If you have not yet chosen a major, write an essay discussing which majors you are considering and why.

how to succeed in the classroom

SETTING GOALS AND MANAGING TIME

We all have goals, some long-term, some immediate, and some in between. Long-term goals are often called "values" and, as I said in the first chapter, most of us want to have successful lives. But that can mean many different things, depending on our talents and more specific goals. I can't speak for you, of course, but I do know that you are in college. That tells me you may have such goals as getting an interesting, well-paying job, meeting a person to marry or have as a partner, having a good time, or developing the talents and interests that will allow you to enjoy life to its fullest and achieve truly worthy objectives. College is a great step toward a successful life.

Goals and values are not just given to us, like our hair color. True, we are shaped by many factors, including our family background, religious tradition, friends, and media. But unlike my dog, Sam, who is in no position to reject her values (she loves to sleep in the sun and lean against people), you and I can reject some of the values we have traditionally accepted. That's what college is about in part—reviewing the values we have assumed are right for us to see if they really are worthwhile. Sam can't ask whether what she wants is really worthwhile or valuable; she just wants some things and not others. So the ability of people to reflect on, modify, and even reject our long-held goals and deepest values is not trivial. It distinguishes humans from other animals.

Another problem we have that Sam doesn't is that we think about how to pursue our larger goals most effectively. For Sam, life is pretty simple. Attending a college, choosing a major, marrying, and studying are not decisions she has to make, which leads me to managing time.

When I was a graduate student, I had a lot of trouble actually sitting down and writing my book-length dissertation for my Ph.D. I still remember the day (before computers) that I bought two dozen legal pads and put them on my desk. Somehow I had to get myself to fill those pads, writing hundreds of pages, and it seemed impossible. I then hit on an idea. I would forget about that book I had to write and focus instead on one week's work. I would write at least 4 pages each day, but if I hadn't written 20 pages by Friday, I would have to work on the weekend until I had written the 20 pages. Then the next Monday I would start again, with my 4 pages per day.

This story has a happy ending. Before long I had written 100 pages, then 100 more, something I thought impossible when staring at the stack of blank legal pads. What was *not* impossible, something I had done many times before, was to write a few pages.

My story contains a lesson that you may find useful. People's goals and values are structured. Some very big ones such as having a successful life, are at the top, but under that are others, including financial security, interesting work, status and respect from others, and love of family and friends. You may also have a goal of becoming a particular type of person: courageous, truthful, religious, honest, or loyal, for example. Achieving those goals in turn suggests other goals. Financial security and job satisfaction will be helped by getting a college degree, for example. So eventually we are led to specific goals, such as passing an exam.

My point is that you should not think just about your larger goals but should also focus on the little ones. Time is infinitely divisible into little bits and achieving our larger, long-term goals is impossible unless we divide those into smaller and smaller ones until, finally, we have something we can do in a reasonably short time. Getting a college degree is a big task, but doing one assignment is not. Yet doing that assignment and others like it, one at a time, is like writing one page of a dissertation. It's not that hard. Fair enough, I can hear you saying, you make it sound easy. I said in Chapter 1 that diligence is important, and now I say it again. But how can people manage to actually do all those little bits, and to do them well, when there are so many other fun things to do? The answer is study habits.

STUDY SKILLS, STUDY HABITS, AND LEARNING STYLES

*P*eople say being a good student has two aspects: natural ability (which people can't control) and effort (which we can). I disagree. Instead of those stark contrasts, I think it's more accurate to say that how well you do in your studies depends on (1) your *study skills* at reading, writing, and analyzing, and (2) your *study habits*, that is, the time and effort you put into classes and how you use that time. Skills as well as habits are partly within your control. While it is true that reading, writing, and analyzing skills are *influenced* by native-born talent, they can also be improved. That much is known; what we don't know is the mix. How much is natural, and how much is learned? But that question doesn't need answering, since it's undoubtedly true that those skills can be significantly improved by working on them. So virtually anybody can be at least a good student, if not a spectacular one.

For some who start out lacking basic study skills, this may require more time and a longer view. But that's in large part what this book is about: trying to help those of you who want to learn to be a good or maybe even a spectacular student. Then, once basic skills are in place, all that's left is to apply them in an efficient, conscientious way to courses. This involves study habits.

Studying is your job as a college student. No surprise there, right? But think about it a minute. The vast majority of people in their late teens and early twenties living in this world (and more than half of all Americans) are working at a full-time job rather than in college. So it's useful to think of studying as a type of employment. You have vacations from being a student, of course, but while working you owe it to yourself and to others to treat your studies with at least as much seriousness as working people treat the plant or firm where they clock in every morning.

Unless you are superhuman, you can't hope to do well in class unless you have good study habits (everybody *has* study habits; the trick is to have *good* ones). Good study habits are the ones that work well for you, which makes it a little difficult—but not quite impossible—to describe what they are for everybody. For one thing, it's almost always a good idea to study in the same place and to do it on a regular schedule. This is especially true for people who sometimes don't quite manage to find the time to get their work done well and on time. So once you know your courses, set up a weekly schedule, write it down, and stick to it no matter what: if this is Monday, from 10:30 to 12:00 noon, for instance, you know you'll be studying no matter what.

It's also important to find the right place to study; obviously, having noise and friends around isn't a good idea. Neither is it smart (as I once did when I was a graduate student) to get in the habit of resting or even sleeping in your study space. Before long, I found it almost impossible to stay awake once I sat down at that green metal desk in the Vanderbilt University Library. But eventually I learned that I had to establish the right associations with that space, which were *not* that I could rest there. Once that happened, I didn't get sleepy. The same goes for eating and talking with friends: keep your study space separate from other activities. Need I add that having TV on makes serious studying impossible?

Other ways to keep focused on your work if you get sleepy or bored are to turn down the heat (warm rooms make people drowsy), get something to drink (caffeineated, if necessary), change what you're studying to something else for a while, or go for a brief walk. Finally, if all else fails, you may in fact need a short nap. It's not the end of the world, especially if you keep your promise to yourself to return to work immediately, but be sure to take it somewhere besides work space! If you find yourself heading to the library or wherever you study and it's a day that you desperately wish you could do something else, try focusing on the fact that once you're there and concentrating on your work, your interest will become focused on that. Tell yourself that while you don't want to work now, once you get into the material, it will be interesting. If that is not true, then you aren't studying the right way.

One final thought about studying and learning: studies show that people differ not just in how *easily* they learn but also in *how they learn most easily*. Some people have great memories. This allows them to pick up foreign languages with ease and to remember all kinds of details about what they are studying. Other people are better at remembering ideas. I'm more in that category. I often remember a distinction or argument a student gave in class or on a paper long after I've forgotten the student's name, the year, and sometimes even the course.

Besides being better at learning some things, such as facts and general ideas, people also differ in *how* they learn best. Some people are good visual learners and can recollect many details of how a room looked, for instance, after they leave it. I once knew a law student who was accused of cheating because he gave the complete legal citations of dozens of cases during an examination. A typical citation is *Railway Express Agency v. New York,*

336 U.S. 106 (1949). He had what is sometimes called a photographic memory and could visualize huge amounts of text on a page. Others learn better by listening and are able to recall information and ideas by thinking about what they heard somebody say or do.

These simple but important facts about different learning styles have implications for your studies, since you can use how you most efficiently learn to your advantage. If you learn better by hearing, for example, then it's especially important to attend lectures and to emphasize talking with teachers, other students, or anybody else about the material. Be sure to see if your professor will let you tape-record classes, if that is helpful. Reading especially difficult material aloud is also good to try. If you are a better visual learner, use that to your advantage by creating outlines of the material to review, visualizing the pages with important information, and making note cards with written questions and answers. You may want to consider other learning tricks. Sometimes when lecturing, for example, I use a key letter from each item in a list I want students to remember to make a word. If students can remember the word, it usually reminds them of each item on the list. Amy did this in law school to remember the elements of "adverse possession" (don't ask). The answer was "open, continuous, hostile, exclusive, actual, and notorious." She remembered those six words as "ocean" except spelled as it sounds: "ochean." Whatever works for you, right?

WHY GO TO CLASS AND DO HOMEWORK ASSIGNMENTS?

*d*epending on the professor, one reason for going to class and completing assignments might be that unless you do, you'll be graded down and counted absent, and your grade will suffer. But there are other, even better reasons for going to class. You'll do better on papers and exams, the professor will get to know you, you will become more adept at speaking to groups, and you'll learn more about the material. Finally, you might also learn something about yourself by participating in discussions, refining what you think about issues, and learning how to interact with people more effectively.

Teachers often say it's especially important that you study the material before coming to class. They also claim that it's even more important in *their* class than in others, something that can't possibly be true in general, any more than everybody can be above average height. Still, the basic point is right: it *is* important to do your work before coming to class. Apart from helping you learn, it's also your responsibility to other students, since it allows the class to move more quickly and avoids wasting everybody's time as the professor explains obvious points to class members who didn't do their work. Finally, it makes professors happy. So let's assume you want to spend the requisite amount of time doing your assignment. The traditional rule is at least two hours outside class for every hour of class time. How can you use this time most wisely, so that you are as well prepared as possible for class, get the most out of class when you are there, and ultimately do well on exams?

Students find assignments difficult for many different reasons. Often there is no getting around the fact that the material is tough. Other times, if you are reading an essay or section of a book, the antiquated writing style, as well as the material itself, may cause problems.

You will have assignments in virtually every course you take in college. As you read and study, keep in mind the author's purpose in writing what you are reading and the professor's goals in having you do the assignment. These can vary from course to course, so it's important to get clearly in mind just why you have been asked to read and study outside of class.

There are basically three different types of assignments, reflecting the objectives that a professor might have in asking students to read and study material. One is to have students learn information and facts; second is to help them learn to solve problems; and third is to help them understand a persuasive essay. I will discuss the first two in the next section, saving how to read essays (and understand what you are reading) for its own chapter. A fourth, common type of assignment is to read a primary source such as a historical document or a work of fiction (a play, poem, or novel). Normally, though, the ultimate point of such assignments falls under one of the first three purposes I mentioned, with the goal to gain information and facts and also to be able to discuss different, often competing arguments and interpretations of what you have read.

LEARNING INFORMATION AND SOLVING PROBLEMS

Often homework involves learning new facts, definitions, and the like. This occurs, in varying degrees, in virtually all courses, though the exact nature of the information will vary widely as will the emphasis put on learning it: some disciplines put much more emphasis on acquisition of information and facts than others, just as some professors also put more or less emphasis on it, even within the same field. For many subjects, it is central. History and the social sciences cannot be studied without a solid grounding in the facts. Before you can intelligently discuss the causes of the Cold War or the role of Lincoln in freeing the slaves, for instance, you need to know lots of facts. Similarly, it's impossible to understand the importance of the U.S. Supreme Court in contemporary politics without lots of background information about American government. The same goes, of course, for the natural sciences. Nobody can hope to grasp chemistry, biology, or physics without first mastering a great deal of factual information. Even mathematics assumes a student understands key concepts and definitions, and discussion of literature cannot even get started until readers have a grasp of the basic characters and events that have taken place in the novel or play.

How then can you best use your time if the purpose of the assignment is for you to learn facts? One excellent study aid is underlining and making notes, either in the margin or, better still, on a separate sheet of paper. Your goal is to sift through all the material and pick out the important facts and definitions. Usually more facts and definitions than you need will be included, so the problem becomes telling the difference between what is important and what is only background. To do that, you need to have a sense of the larger purposes the author (and, by implication, the professor) wants to accomplish. Why is it important, in other words, for you to learn these facts? What purpose are they serving?

One purpose of learning facts is linked to the second general purpose of class assignments I mentioned: problem solving. When I teach logic, for example, the ultimate point of reading and understanding the information in the chapters is to be able to solve the problems by showing how to deduce the conclusion from the premises. Science, and especially math, classes also will often involve problem solving.

Sometimes in class, you may feel you understand something, but that can be very misleading. Though sitting in class you may be able to follow how the teacher is solving a problem, when you are on your own with the book you may not be able to do it. This distinction is important. You will need to be able not just to follow along as somebody else solves a problem but also to do it yourself. That can be much more difficult.

How then should you proceed when given a set of problems to solve? First review your notes from class and study carefully and slowly the explanatory material you have been assigned. Without that, you have little chance of being able to do the problems. Often you will be provided a definition of terms and perhaps some examples. It is very helpful, if not essential, for you to be able to "see" intuitively what something means or why something works. Simply memorizing, without understanding, is not enough.

Then turn to the problems. Normally the harder ones come later, so start at the beginning. Sometimes, too, you will encounter a series of the same type of problem, so that once you can do that type, you can move on to the next. Remember that there is no substitute for practice if your goal is learning how to solve problems. The more problems you do, the better you will learn. It helps to try to solve them by yourself first, without looking at answers in the book. It's easy to think you know how to do something just because you can follow along when somebody else does it. But just as when you are hiking, following somebody else is not the same thing as getting there yourself. So don't be misled into thinking you can learn the easy way, without actually struggling to find the answer on your own.

PARTICIPATING IN CLASS DISCUSSIONS

*b*esides giving different types of assignments, professors conduct classes in different ways; sometimes even the same professor may want to lecture one day and have an open-ended discussion with lots of student participation the next. Usually, though, if a professor is lecturing—that is, explaining what is in the book or supplementing it with other material—you can still ask questions. You can usually tell if the instructor wants questions or would rather wait until finishing a point. If you can't tell, ask after class.

Classes may seem a strangely artificial form of discussion, with people coming hazy from a previous late night to argue about Kant or the morality of euthanasia at 9 o'clock in the morning. But at its best, class discussion can be enjoyable and a fantastic learning experience; ideas seem to spark off others, with a range of alternative viewpoints displayed clearly and sometimes even memorably. The success or failure of a discussion depends partly on the skills of the professor, but it also depends on you and your fellow students. Class discussion presents an opportunity for students to take initiative, using the skills and knowledge of the instructor and their own to assist in their learning.

When having discussions, professors always appreciate students who participate actively and intelligently. (But don't, *do not,* sit for a long time with your hand up, after it is clear the professor knows you have a question. Put it down, and wait until a better moment to raise it again.) Remember that students' comments do not have to be brilliant; I find that sometimes even a simple, straightforward request to explain a point is immensely helpful. So don't make the mistake of thinking that your question or comment isn't worthwhile; it's rare for only one student in a class to be confused. In any case, what seems to you to be evidence of your own confusion can in fact turn out to be a profoundly serious objection to what's being discussed. It's impossible to know, without asking, how important and insightful your comment or question may be—and you may not know even after you've raised it. But then, that's what discussions are often like.

Here are some suggestions about how to succeed in, and enjoy, class discussions.

1. Be sure you've studied the material before you ask a question. It's usually obvious to professors—and to other students—when you haven't done your homework or read the assigned material.

2. Before coming to class, think about what is on *your* agenda—the points you want to make and the questions you would like discussed. It is up to you to raise them.

3. Don't make comments just to impress the professor, or the person sitting next to you for that matter. It usually doesn't work to ask questions unless something is genuinely puzzling, confusing, or worrying you.

4. Avoid dominating the discussion, even if you know more about the material or issues than the other students do. Discussions belong to everybody.

5. Follow the thread of the argument by listening to what other students say rather than riding your own hobbyhorse. Personal anecdotes are rarely helpful in classes and usually waste time or, worse, lead the discussion astray. Learn to stay on the point.

6. Acknowledge other students' contributions, both through eye contact and by referring back to them (for example, "the point that Mary made about XYZ"). Be especially sensitive in the case of fellow students who appear shy.

7. If you are shy yourself, there are some simple ways to join the discussion without immediately exposing yourself to the risk that you will be challenged or ridiculed. You could respond to someone else's contribution with a comment like, "That's an interesting point that I had not thought about in that way before. Could you please expand on it?" Or you might ask how a previous speaker might respond to a comment that another student just made.

8. If you are preparing a formal classroom presentation, make sure it is punchy and brief. Use your notes, but do not read them. Don't think of this as an opportunity to show how clever and hard working you are; instead, try to engage your fellow students in a constructive discussion of the topic. Finally, once you have introduced the topic, don't just sit back and expect the professor to take over without further help from you. Remember: if you initiated it, you're the one responsible for leading the discussion.

Keep in mind that class discussion is one of the best ways to learn. Besides making yourself known to the professor, you'll find that you remember material much better if you've actively participated in discussions. Exciting, intense class discussions with students can be like other collective activities, such as a first-rate symphony concert or an unusually well-played sporting event. If successful, all of the participants can be proud of their achievement. Nobody could have achieved it without the talent and cooperation of the others.

TAKING GOOD NOTES IN CLASS: WHY AND HOW

*j*ust as it's important to read carefully and skillfully in preparation for class, so too is it important to attend class actively and to take good notes. Never sit passively in class, mindlessly watching what's going on or, worse, daydreaming or sleeping. Force yourself to be active: take notes, think about whether you agree with what's being said, and imagine how you might respond to what the professor or other students are saying.

Note taking, whether done in class or while reading, is a skill. That means you can be better or worse at it, and that you can also get better with thought and practice. Most importantly, keep in mind what the lecturer wants to accomplish: is it to explain specific information and facts, or is it to present different sides of an issue or a single argument or interpretation of something? Your goal is to figure out and then capture in your notes what the lecturer is trying to convey.

I suggest using what is often called the Cornell system of note taking, developed by Walter Pauk at Cornell University. This system uses three parts. First, on the right side of the paper, take notes in the normal, outline format. Second, leave a "cue column" on the left of the page to use later as you review the notes. This area can include your own comments and thoughts as well as memory aids or examples. Third, allow some space at the bottom of the page so you can make a brief summary of what is on the page.

Some professors use PowerPoint (a software for making presentations), so give some thought to how to take notes when that happens. Don't automatically take down everything that is shown or ignore what is not. You need to think about what's important, just as with a regular lecture. You can also ask the professor for advice on taking notes. I recommend using loose-leaf paper, so that you can then put the pages into a binder. If you miss a class, you can borrow somebody else's notes and put them where they belong. Loose-leaf paper is relatively cheap. If you use loose-leaf, you won't have wasted paper left at the end of notebooks after a course ends.

Here are some more specific suggestions for taking notes.

1. Come to class prepared by having studied the reading assignment. This allows you to follow the lecture more easily and concentrate on the details of what's being said.

2. At the beginning of class, write at the top of each page the name of the class and the date; then number the pages linked to the date. (For instance, you might have 9/22A, 9/22B, 9/22C, and so on.)

3. Focus on the big picture: the structure or pattern of the lecture (or discussion, if there is one) is what you most want to capture in your notes. Keep in mind that you are trying to capture what matters, not the inessential stuff. Writing down what's important should keep you pretty busy in itself.

4. Don't mindlessly write down material you already know. Remember: you're looking for what's new.

5. Take notes in outline form, organized around major topics and themes. Even if you don't use the Cornell system, leave space between topics for use later, either to fill in after class or while you are studying.

6. After class, before your memory fades, take a few minutes to review the notes briefly and fill in missing parts.

7. Learn to use abbreviations. It's good to make a list of the ones you use and then add to it as you proceed. Here are a few general abbreviations you may find helpful.

bc	=	because
R	=	reason
wrt	=	with regard to
esp	=	especially
w/	=	with
w/o	=	without
$\therefore$		therefore
$\rightarrow$	=	leads to or implies
$>$	=	more or greater than
$<$	=	fewer or less than
$=$	=	same as or equal to

It's also efficient note-taking practice to omit vowels when writing or to replace them with something shorter: "becz u lrnd shrthnd u cn tk bttr nts." Different courses will invite their own abbreviations, depending on the subject matter. Use abbreviations you develop yourself, usually the first few letters of the word. You will often easily know the meaning from the context—for instance, abo = abortion; rel = religion; soc = Socrates. You get the picture.

ADDITIONAL SUGGESTIONS: JOURNALS, STUDY GROUPS, AND REVIEW QUESTIONS

*h*ere are a few more useful hints about studying. First, you should think about keeping a *journal* in which you record your reactions to the readings, lectures, and class discussions. While this is no substitute for aggressively reading and taking careful notes on the material in the way I have described, it can serve worthy purposes. First, it helps focus attention on what *you* think is important, an experience that can stand you in good stead during class discussions. Second, a journal often helps make the material come alive and thus more interesting to you personally. Finally, when you finish the course, you'll have a record of your reactions to the material to keep for the future as sort of an intellectual diary. Often these journals make interesting reading for you (or others) later in life.

Most important, I believe, is studying with other students. While attending class is usually necessary, there's good evidence that the students who most enjoy college and who report getting the most out of their classes not only study hard but, even *more* importantly, also are involved in intellectual activities taking place outside the classroom. Harvard University has published the *Harvard Assessment Seminars,* designed to look at what works and what doesn't in educating students. This is what the study concluded:

> There is common wisdom at many colleges that the best advice for students, in addition to just attending classes and doing homework, is: Get involved. Get involved in campus activities of all sorts [such as sports, student government, fraternities, sororities, and various clubs]. . . . But there is a different kind of involvement, a more subtle kind, and the undergraduates who are both happiest academically and most successful stress its importance. Nearly without exception, these students have at least one, and often more than one, intense relationship *built around academic work with other people.* Some have it with a professor. Others have it with an advisor. Some build it with a group of fellow students outside the classroom. The critical point is that the relationship is not merely social. It is organized to accomplish some work. (emphasis in original)[1]

---

[1]Richard J. Light, *Harvard Assessment Seminars* (Cambridge: Harvard Graduate School of Education, 1990).

This study is striking. It suggests that discussions outside class with fellow students and others, which are often thought of as a relatively unimportant part of college compared with homework and classroom participation, are in fact the most significant factor shaping how much students learn and whether they enjoy their experience in college.

To take advantage of this finding, I strongly suggest (and sometimes also require) that my students develop these sorts of relationships not just with me but with one another. Besides keeping my own office hours and assigning joint projects in which students prepare and make class presentations among themselves, it's valuable for students just to meet among themselves, informally outside of the classroom, to discuss the readings, class discussion, lectures, and assignments. Sometimes I require that students set a regular time and meet weekly for at least an hour throughout the semester, often with others in the class they have never met. I ask them to keep a journal of these meetings in which they record the time, date, and topics discussed, followed by their own reactions to the meetings. Often students report that these meetings are the most rewarding time they spend on the class.

A successful study group may be as small as you and a friend, roommate, or study partner. But don't think the only person you can learn anything from is a student who seems to be doing better than you. Every professor will tell you that the students who talk the most or ask the most questions are not necessarily the ones who do the best work. Furthermore, explaining material to others is one of the surest ways to master it yourself. The most important thing is that you meet and that you talk seriously about the material.

Finally, many textbooks include review and discussion questions, which are useful in a variety of ways. Sometimes it's worthwhile to look at them *before* you read the assignment, in order to help focus your attention on the material. Or you can take a few minutes after you have done the assignment to see if you can answer the questions. Keep in mind that some of the questions will be mainly expository and others critical or comparative. As a general rule, if you can answer these questions correctly, you've gotten the drift of the assigned reading; if not, you haven't.

Review Questions and Exercises

1. Write a short essay in which you set out your goals for the current academic year. Be as specific as possible.
2. Keep a time diary for 24 hours, in which you describe how you spend each 15-minute segment. Explain briefly what you learned from this exercise. Were you surprised by what you discovered?

3. What is wrong with the idea that how well people do in college is determined by natural ability and effort? How does the author suggest that study skills and study habits shape success?

4. Describe the different learning styles.

5. Write a short essay explaining which of the different learning styles most accurately describes you. Then discuss the different learning techniques and identify which ones should work best for you.

6. What is the Cornell note-taking method?

the care and feeding of professors

PROFESSORS ARE PEOPLE, TOO

It's true—professors are people, too. And like students, we come in about a million different shapes, sizes, and teaching styles. Some professors (like me) tend to get excited in class, while others are more calm and careful; some like to call on students, while others take only volunteers; some have lots of class participation and discussion that encourage students to develop and defend their own viewpoints, while others prefer to spend more time lecturing, making sure students have understood the material and providing students with the professor's perspective on the readings; some professors stand still or sit, while others move around the room waving their arms; some rely on notes or an outline, while others speak more from memory. The point is that there isn't really a one-size-fits-all way to teach.

Most professors I've come across care a great deal about teaching. But that said, it's also the case that no single approach or teaching style works best for everybody. If you're smart, you'll try to figure out how you can get the most from the particular professors you have. It's rare to find a professor whose style can't enable students to learn; the trick is to learn how to learn from, and to take advantage of, the strengths of all your teachers. If discussion is central, then participation is important. If the professor lectures but is not very exciting, that creates its own problem (staying awake), which brings me to the next subject.

HINTS FOR GETTING ALONG WITH PROFESSORS

*i*t is important to keep in mind that professors notice what students do and say in class. Although when it comes time to evaluate a student's work, we may try to ignore the fact that a student slept through class or was absent much of the time, why put yourself in that position? Remember: professors are people too. Here are some suggestions for getting along with your professors.

First, remember that we are trying to make the class interesting to you and to help you learn, but you have to do your part. For one thing, never, ever, go to sleep in class. I'm sure you already know that, but you'd be surprised how often I hear about it happening and sometimes see it in my own classes. I remember a class at Harvard Law School in which some of the students made a habit of reading newspapers in class. Don't think professors don't notice. Such behavior is distracting at best and discouraging and embarrassing at worst. If you're tired, have a soda or a cup of coffee or tea; even ask your teacher if it's OK to bring some to class. Another possibility if you find yourself tired or bored is to promise yourself that you will ask a question or make a comment of some sort within the next 10 minutes. It's hard to relax with that over your head! Or, if all else fails, you should ask to leave the room. Even that's better than sleeping.

Professors also notice facial expressions. Students who seem attentive, showing agreement, disagreement, or even puzzlement, are better off than ones who show nothing or, worse, boredom. Seeing that people are bored by what you're saying is disheartening to anybody, even professors. We also notice when a student is reading something while class is going on, so don't do that either. Also, it's usually pretty easy to tell from an open book whether a student has read the day's assignment: almost nobody reads these days without marking up the text. Finally, don't misspell the professor's name on papers or exams. It really jumps off the page, and it happens more often than you might think.

One more suggestion: don't say to a professor that you don't like a paper you wrote, that you had to do it in a hurry, or that you didn't have time to prepare adequately for an exam. It's the professor's job to assess your work. Comments like those don't excuse bad work, and they might even hurt your grade by subconsciously influencing the professor to read more critically. Like I said, professors are people too.

Sometimes I hear it said that it's good for students to make themselves known personally to professors by coming to office hours (periods of time reserved to talk with students informally in the professor's office), for instance, or by speaking after class. I can't speak for others, but that has never seemed to me to be important or even helpful. Most professors try to be fair and objective and to not let personal feelings affect their grading. What's more, if you do that and it is obvious you don't have a good reason to be there, then it can have just the opposite effect. My advice is to do whatever seems natural. If you have a reason to speak with a teacher, then do it; otherwise, don't. Don't do it with an ulterior motive.

Students sometimes wonder if, and for how long, they should go to office hours. This can be a bit tricky since a professor's situation can vary from class to class and professor to professor. Obviously, though, if there is a long line and you can tell a professor is busy, don't go in if all you want to do is chat or introduce yourself. Save that for another time, when things have settled down. Also, some professors may appreciate you coming even if you have nothing in particular to ask, while others may not. Here again you'll have to make that judgment on a case-by-case basis.

You might be surprised by how much professors worry about classes, including students and their problems. These problems can range from students who are disruptive (and sometimes even violent) to minor problems involving students who talk too much, or too little, during discussions to personal problems that affect a student's work. Some of these problems, such as illness, are inevitable; others can be avoided. Here are some suggestions for dealing with the unavoidable ones and for avoiding the self-destructive ones.

If you must miss class due to illness, for instance, or a death in the family, always let the professor know about it—preferably *before* you miss class. When you do, explain the problem briefly and ask if there is anything special you should do. Indicate that you plan to get the notes and do whatever assignments you may miss. If you don't know anybody in the class, ask the professor if he would ask a student to let you copy notes. If you will miss a due date for a paper or a test, be prepared to set a date when you will complete the assignment. Try to be flexible if you can, but be sure to set up a specific date. It is in *your* interest to have a firm deadline. And don't lie or make up excuses. Sometimes professors will ask for documentation, in which case you may get caught lying. Even if you are not caught, it's wrong to lie, and you know it (or should). If you have missed a class and have not been able to understand something, you should make a short visit during your professor's office hours. But come only after you have tried hard to understand the material on your own and have read the notes you borrowed. Come with specific questions. That way, the professor will know you are trying hard on your own.

Do keep in mind that professors have different teaching loads and other responsibilities at various times. What might work in a semester when a professor has only small classes would be impossible if the class has hundreds of students. So think about that when you ask for special help, different test dates, and other special consideration. Even just letting the professor know you are aware of the problem can help, especially if the professor is also responsible for hundreds of other students.

As for telephoning, most professors make a fairly sharp distinction between calls (or e-mails) to the office, which are OK, and phone calls at home (which generally are not a good idea). There can be exceptions, of course, and some professors will be more tolerant than others. (We once got a call well after midnight from a student wondering about a grade, which did not make Amy happy at all.)

THE RECOMMENDATION QUESTION

Sometimes students ask for a recommendation from me as if I were doing them a favor. Though the occasional professor may think of writing for students as an extra burden, I think we should see it as part of our job, like showing up for classes and grading exams. Whatever attitude you confront, you will need to deal with it. Sometimes that's easy, especially if you know the professor well and have a relaxed, friendly relationship. In that case, I'd just ask (well in advance of the due date) if your teacher would be willing to write for you and ask what, if any, additional information the professor might need. It's more difficult if you don't know the professor well; perhaps the class was large or you rarely spoke up in discussions. But the only solution is, again, to ask.

Which professor should you ask? In general, ask the ones who know you best. It is difficult to write a letter if the only class I had with a student is a large one. Smaller classes and seminars are best. I would not necessarily choose the professor who gave you the highest grade. Some professors give everybody high grades, and, in any case, the grade you got is only one small part of the recommendation. Good references are specific rather than general and speak to the particular strengths of the student. So the better the person knows you, the better the recommendation will be.

I find it very helpful in writing recommendations (I usually write from 50 to 100 per year) if I have available in one place all the relevant information about the student. I have a form that I give students who want me to write for them that asks them to provide me with the following information in a folder with their name on it: what the recommendation is for (graduate school, law or medical school, a job); a resume, if they have one; a list of the classes the student took with me, including the semester and final grade; a copy of the student's transcript; copies of papers the student wrote for me (especially if I have made positive comments on them); a copy of the student's personal statement that is to be included in the application to professional or graduate school; and a summary of any other information the student thinks is relevant. I emphasize that it is important to be as helpful as possible, which means including everything that I might be able to use.

Though modesty is a virtue, this is not the time to show it or to assume your professor will remember everything. A short reminder of some conversation you had with the professor or of something unusual that happened in class is often very useful to me. Most professors want to write a good recommendation for students, and your job is to help us do it. Again, this is no time for modesty.

Even if your professor does not ask for specific information, I'd suggest you include it along with anything else that is requested. I ask for all of that from students when they first approach me to write a letter. It's a good idea for you either to come with that available when you ask or to volunteer to provide it. Be sure to provide envelopes with the address on them where the recommendation should be sent (and with the *professor's* return address, not your own). Since the professor rarely, if ever, will have to pay postage, I don't think it's necessary to include a stamp. But some students do, and it's not a bad idea to offer if you are uncertain.

Finally, it is important for you to agree not to look at the recommendation, and to indicate that you have agreed on the form, if it asks. That way, readers can know the recommendation was honest. If you are supposed to include the recommendation with your application, ask the professor to seal it in an envelope and to sign across the seal. That way, the recommendation's objectivity cannot be questioned.

PROBLEM PROFESSORS

i tend to think of the rules governing classroom behavior as a kind of social contract: if students come to class prepared, are attentive and in their seats on time, don't talk out of turn during class (except when we're all talking or joking), and produce good work, then I will do all

I can to be sure the time we spend is never wasted, that the material is exciting and interesting, and that students are graded fairly. That contractualist approach is not a bad one for you to take as well. If, despite conscientious effort, you're having trouble getting through all the work, a deadline for a paper is too short, or the material is being covered too quickly or too slowly, you should make your feelings known. Don't make a big deal of it, and don't try to embarrass the professor in class by complaining publicly. Just ask for help in addressing the problem. It's always best to assume that a professor will be reasonable, at least until you're proven wrong.

There are, however, some professors who are not reasonable or fair. I knew one who simply refused to talk to students about how he determined grades, and another who insisted that all students line up at a precise time for office hours. He would leave if nobody was there at the exact hour. I also know of professors who have the reputation of grading students who disagree with them more harshly. Also, the familiar problems of sexual harassment and discrimination exist at every university. It's a safe bet your college or university has a published policy governing these and other matters. So before doing anything, I'd look at the rules. Ask for a copy of whatever material is available describing the rights and responsibilities of faculty and of students, and read it. Next you should go to the professor, not to prove what you have learned but to see if you can work something out. Point out the relevant policy, and explain why you think you were not treated properly. Perhaps it was only a misunderstanding, or maybe the professor didn't know about the policy. It's best to resolve matters informally if you can.

What if, despite all your efforts at being reasonable, you are still persuaded you have not been treated properly? Your next step would be to go higher up, normally to the chair of the department. Rules govern professors' conduct and ensure that students are treated fairly; administrators are there to enforce the rules. The college will probably also have a process whereby you can appeal grades, usually to other faculty, as well as an administrator charged with dealing with harassment and discrimination. All this is difficult, stressful, and time consuming, so proceed advisedly. Nevertheless, students do have rights: the classroom is not an autocracy ruled by a lawless despot. You are entitled to receive fair, impartial treatment from conscientious professors who do their jobs.

On a positive note, most professors in my experience want to be helpful and fair and definitely *do* appreciate it when students communicate problems they are having getting work done. This is especially true when the communication comes well before something is due. Never wait until after a deadline has passed. Even if you hope you might be able to get an assignment done on time, let the professor know what your problem is and that it might be late. That way, the professor knows you are concerned about getting the work done and on schedule.

Even though we hear all kinds of excuses, some more creative than others, it's rare for a professor to be unwilling to make exceptions when there's good reason to do so. But, as I said earlier, don't ever lie about having a good reason, such as illness. It's wrong. Most students are not good liars, and students who lie also make it harder for themselves and others when a real emergency arises. Again, it's best to assume that people will treat you fairly.

Review Questions and Exercises

1. Write an essay explaining what you hope to accomplish in your classes. How will you try to achieve those goals?

2. Write an essay describing what you think an ideal student would be. Then discuss how close you think you are to that ideal student.

3. Go to one of your professors' office hours or make an appointment. While there, ask the professor what he or she hopes to accomplish in the class, and why the professor chose teaching as a career. Then write a short essay discussing your reaction to what the professor said, and whether or not the discussion made you more interested in teaching as a career.

logic and critical thinking

THE TOOLS OF THE TRADE

WHAT IS REASONING AND WHY DOES IT MATTER?

Much of what goes on in universities and colleges involves reasoning, whether it's developing and defending our own ideas or understanding and assessing somebody else's. We reason with one another, for example, about how nature works, what society is like, or how we ought to act. It's usually good that we do reason, considering the alternatives. Logic and critical thinking are aspects of the field that studies reasoning—in particular, how to distinguish good reasoning from bad. It is a complex, fascinating subject, and I will only scratch the surface here. But in my experience, even a brief introduction to critical thinking and logic is useful to students. It enables them to become more aware of reasoning processes and more adept at making good arguments as well as avoiding being fooled by bad ones. It also helps, as you will see, in understanding precisely what is being claimed—what something means—and also in noticing when meaning is unclear. So my goal in this chapter is to give you some tools that can make you a better (more logical) reasoner, whether as a reader, discussant, or writer.

First, I want to say something about reasoning in general, and its relationship to logic and critical thinking. Universities are wonderful places: even the U.S. Supreme Court has held so. University faculty, and students, are protected by the U.S. Constitution to speak their minds without fear of reprisal. But before you tee off against an administration's policies, you might want to keep in mind that such freedoms are not absolute. Private institutions have more authority to restrict speech than do state-run ones, and there are always limits on the time, place, and manner of speech, even if what you say is otherwise constitutionally protected. Though you are entitled to express your opinions about most everything, you can't do it by spray-painting a building or disrupting a classroom. Nevertheless, both students and faculty do enjoy broad First Amendment protection, which allows us to say unpopular and even offensive things to one another without fear of reprisal. (That same First Amendment also protects those who disagree with you, however, so don't be surprised if you get back as good as—or even better than—you give!) Universities are therefore inherently controversial and divisive places where ideas are tried out, criticized, defended, and sometimes ridiculed.

Why encourage all this ferment, debate, and arguing? The answer, of course, is that we learn from it. Testing theories about how nature works, developing new ways of interpreting the world, and offering new philosophical, historical, and other ideas about human life and societies all rely on the availability of criticisms and commentaries. We can proceed no other way, at least not very effectively. Reasoning with one another, in the broad sense of proposing ideas and theories for discussion and criticism, is the heart of a university: we can't ultimately know if what we are saying is true or good or valuable unless we are lucky enough to attract critical attention. But not all attention is helpful, of course, and that's where reason comes in. Somebody who burns a book or screams epithets at a speaker is probably enjoying the attention, but at the end of the day that's not nearly as helpful as offering thoughtful criticism based on reasons. We learn from such outbursts that the person is offended or angry, not whether the person is entitled to be.

If I am right, and free speech and debate exercised in the service of reason are at the heart of a university, then what is reason? Begin with the idea of an argument, not in the sense of things people *have with* one another, but in the sense of things that we *give to* one another. To give an argument is to give reasons for a conclusion. Reasons are given to change people's beliefs, though there are other ways to change people's beliefs as well. For example, you may not believe it is a good idea for me to say you were wrong until I produce a pistol. That threat, however, is not an argument—at least not in the sense that we use the term. Besides threats of force, reasons should also be distinguished from (mere) emotional appeals and rhetoric. Suppose two people give word for word the same talk defending, for example, affirmative action or global warming, but one does so with great emotional appeal and the other simply reads the speech coldly, without feeling. Has the first given any better reason to believe the conclusion? No. Will the first be more persuasive? Probably. My point is that the sense of "reasoning" I have in mind is normative—that is, it is concerned not with what actually works to persuade people but with what *should* work. Reasoning is about what people *should* believe, based on evidence. That's why, although it may be easier, and even kinder, to lie and praise a friend's argument, in another sense it is less friendly. If, for example, a friend's paper has mistakes in it then you are not giving your friend advice that will help get to the truth (or a good grade, for that matter).

If reasoning is what we want to do, and inherent in reasoning is a distinction between good and bad ways to persuade people, then how do we know when reasoning is "good" or "bad?"

The answer is logic. All disciplines, whether economics, philosophy, history, or whatever, share one thing. It is not *what* they study, or even the method they use. What they all share is the goal of giving arguments, which means they depend on the norms or rules that we call "rationality." Indeed, every time people try to understand or explain something, they assume that there is an important difference between good reasons or explanations and bad ones. Otherwise, why would anybody bother to study a subject? We might as well just speculate about the answer to a question, or just make up an answer. *Logic* is the name we give to standards and principles of rationality and rational inquiry. All rational inquiry depends on logic.

Why bother to study logic? There are many reasons, but I will mention just two. First, it enables us to learn a great deal about our own language. Like all other spoken languages, English words and sentences are full of ambiguity. Different words can mean different things, as can different sentences. Translating English sentences into precise logical statements helps people appreciate the complexity of their language and to become more adept at saying just what they mean. Second, it is worthwhile to study logic because it helps people reason better. Learning and applying the rules that mark the difference between good and bad reasoning is helpful in analyzing what we hear or read and in formulating our own arguments and reasoning.

I will begin to answer this question by discussing the nature of an argument, including the difference between deductive and inductive arguments. Then I will discuss critical thinking by looking at the most common types of bad reasoning, usually termed "fallacies," which can often lead people to believe something they shouldn't. I will conclude the chapter with a brief introduction to deductive logic.

THE NATURE OF ARGUMENTS

*m*aking and challenging arguments is what we do when we are reasoning. Arguments are offered or disputed in order to persuade people, and good arguments are ones that *should* persuade while bad ones *should not*. But what is an argument? The answer is in the form of *statements, premises,* and *conclusions*.

Let's begin with the nature of language. It helps to think of language as a box of tools enabling us to accomplish a wide variety of goals. But notice how many different things we do with language besides trying to say what is true. Sometimes we may use language to give a warning, for instance, when a friend yells "Look out!" as a car speeds toward you. Other times we use language to express our feelings—for example, by saying "Ouch"—or even to perform an action—such as when a person says "I do" during a marriage ceremony. On other occasions, we may use language to pray or to sing songs or to make promises. The list goes on and on. But much of the time, when we use language, we are trying to say something that is either true or false. We are making a statement of fact. By "fact" here, I don't mean just scientific fact, but anything that we want another person to believe. It could be anything from "Grass is green" or "I like coffee" to "Abortion is murder." Let's call this use of language—where we are saying something that is true or false in the broadest sense—a *statement*.

Arguments are statements, but not just any old group will do. They have a certain form or structure because they comprise at least one premise and one conclusion. A *premise* of an argument, then, is a statement or claim of a particular sort, namely one that is supposed to provide good reason to believe another statement or claim, the *conclusion*. So an *argument* therefore is at least two statements: a premise and a conclusion.

But how do we know which is the premise and which is the conclusion? The answer depends on the meaning and the context. Premises are often shown by *premise indicators*, such as "because," "for the reason," and "since." Conclusions can often be identified by *conclusion indicators*, such as "hence," "therefore," "it follows that," or even "in conclusion." But these indicators are not always there, and so there is no substitute in identifying arguments and their structure for reading, listening, and thinking carefully about what is meant. There is therefore lots of room for argument about the nature of arguments themselves.

Once we notice arguments, we see that they surround us. We think about, analyze, are given, and give arguments all the time. So, for instance, I might say

It rained just recently. I know because the streets are wet.

The conclusion of the argument is that it rained recently; the premise is that the streets are wet. Sometimes the premise or premises are stated first, but sometimes later, as in this example. You can't begin to understand an argument until you know the meaning of what is said, including which statements are premises and which is the conclusion. That's the first step.

But notice, also, that the argument I just gave has another, unstated premise—namely, that the streets being wet makes it certain, or at least more likely, that it has rained recently. That distinction, between arguments claiming to justify a conclusion beyond doubt and ones that only make the conclusion more likely to be true, is the difference between deduction and induction. We will take up those issues shortly.

So we often give an argument without explicitly stating all the premises. We even sometimes don't state the conclusion, as in the following:

The movie will be boring, and anyway I am tired.

Here the missing statement is the conclusion: that we should not go to the movie.

Arguments are also sometimes presented in a linked series, like a chain. This is almost always the case in longer passages and whole essays. In that case, the link between premises and conclusions is not direct, such as the one about wet streets, but instead involves intermediate steps. Consider, for instance, this argument:

Global warming is a problem. We can see from our own experience this summer that the planet is getting warmer. Because of the heat, there is drought and, ultimately, starvation.

This argument is more interesting than the rain one. First, it shows clearly what I said a moment ago: that the first step in understanding an argument is to understand what is meant by its different parts. We often have to read and think carefully about language in order to even recognize an argument, let alone assess its merit. The ultimate conclusion in the global warming argument—what we are asked to believe—is that global warming is a problem. Two premises, according to the argument, justify the conclusion: that the planet is getting warmer and that increased temperatures cause drought and starvation. But notice also that embedded in the argument is still another, subsidiary argument: that we have reason to believe the planet is getting warmer (intermediate conclusion) because we have had a hot summer. In other words, the statement that we have reason to believe the planet is getting warmer does double duty: it is both a premise, supporting the ultimate conclusion that global warming is a problem, and a conclusion that is based on the premise that the summer is getting hotter. As with the first argument, here too we can see that it contains unstated premises. Making those explicit is essential in understanding and ultimately in assessing an argument. So here, then, is an interpretation of the arguments embedded in those three sentences. (There could be others, and you might want to think about whether or not you agree with my interpretation.)

FIRST ARGUMENT:

Premise: This is been a hot summer.

Intermediate conclusion: The planet is getting warmer.

CONCLUDING ARGUMENT:

Premise 1: The planet is getting warmer. (This is also the conclusion of the first argument.)

Premise 2: Warming of the planet is causing drought and, ultimately, starvation.

Final conclusion: Global warming is a problem.

So what have we said so far? That arguments are defined as at least two statements, one of which is a premise and the other a conclusion; that statements are forms of language in which we make a claim that something is true or false; and that premises and conclusions are often identified by indicator words, such as "because," "since," and "therefore."

Keep in mind that the logical test of an argument depends on the relationship between the premises and the conclusion: do those premises, if true, give good reason for accepting the truth of the conclusion? There are two types of arguments because there are two forms that this "good" relationship between premises and conclusion can take. Sometimes the premises, if true, give good but less than conclusive evidence for the conclusion. These arguments are termed *inductive* ones. They rely on patterns and other similarities to give us reasons to believe what we might otherwise not be able to know. So, for example:

Premise: Most lakes in this region are polluted.

Conclusion: Lake James is probably polluted.

(This argument has a hidden premise: that James is a lake in this region.)

But notice that though this is a good argument, another type of argument would establish the same conclusion with greater certainty, assuming its premises were true.

Premise: All lakes in this region are polluted.

Conclusion: Lake James is polluted.

The first type of valid argument, where the conclusion does not follow conclusively and with certainty, is termed "inductive," while the second type, where the premises guarantee the conclusion, is "deductive." If the premises of a deductive argument are (or were) true, then the conclusion must (or would) absolutely have to be true. With inductive arguments, however, the premises only make it likely or probable that the conclusion is true. Inductive arguments can therefore be *stronger* or *weaker,* while deductive ones are more like a light switch or a math problem: they are either right (*valid* is the term logicians use) or they are wrong (*invalid*). Unlike inductive arguments, in deductive ones the conclusion does not "go beyond" the premises.

Unlike deductive ones, inductive arguments, even if very strong, leave open at least the theoretical possibility that the conclusion is false while the premises are true. My belief that you will not win the $100 million lottery with your one ticket is very well justified inductively. But the trick with inductive arguments is to know how strong they are, that is, the degree to which the premises justify the conclusion. The fact that I have won five consecutive bets at the racetrack by itself gives little reason to think I will win the next bet. You'd want to know, for instance, whether I am a novice who just got lucky or an expert who has found a good way to predict a horse's success.

As you may have guessed, inductive arguments are common and come in many forms. Here are four of the most typical types of inductive arguments.

- *Generalizations,* in which, for instance, we infer from a sample of people what the attitudes of all the people in the group are.

- *Predictions,* for example, of weather.

- *Causal inferences,* in which, for example, we conclude that cancer is caused by smoking.

■ *Analogies,* in which we say, for instance, that abortion is acceptable because it is like getting something back that you own (your body) from somebody who has gotten to use it without your permission.[1]

Those examples can be generalized. What follows are more abstract, formal examples of the four types of inductive arguments.

GENERALIZATION:

Premise 1: Very few As are also B.

Premise 2: x is an A.

Conclusion: So x is probably not B.

PREDICTION:

Premise: In the past, when I have done X, then Y has followed.

Conclusion: If I do X now, Y will likely follow.

CAUSAL INFERENCE:

Premise 1: More people in this area have characteristic C than is normal.

Premise 2: People in this area have been exposed to D at higher than normal levels.

Conclusion: Exposure to D causes C.

ANALOGY:

Premise 1: Everything I have examined with characteristics A, B, C, D, and E is also a Q.

Premise 2: t has characteristics A, B, C, D, and E.

Conclusion: t is also probably a Q.

These arguments will be either strong or weak, depending on the specific details of the argument that are given. Probability theory and statistics are the branches of mathematics that are central to inductive reasoning. In standard cases of inductive generalization and other uses of statistical sampling, for instance, the larger the sample (and the more randomly it is chosen) the better. Back to the racetrack example, the more races I have predicted, the better the evidence you have about my next bet being right. Similarly, asking a small number of people who they voted for is not as good a predictor of an election as asking a large group, and asking people only in a heavily Democratic district is not as good as asking a cross section of the population.

---

[1]Judith Thomson uses this analogy in Judith Jarvis Thomson, "A Defense of Abortion," *Philosophy and Public Affairs,* vol. 1, no. 1 (1971): pp. 47–66.

Another important issue in inductive logic involves causal inferences. We need to know, sometimes desperately, whether something in the environment is causing illness or whether it is just a "statistical accident." Statistical accidents do occur: imagine taking a bag of pennies and dumping them on the floor. It's virtually certain you would find some of them grouped together. So when residents of a town have a higher-than-average incidence of cancer, there are always two possible explanations: either something we want to know about is causing the higher incidence, such as water pollution, or it's just a statistical anomaly, like the coins bunched together. Similar issues arise in trying to determine when discrimination is present. Is the higher death rate among babies of one particular ethnic group due to prejudice and therefore poorer care given by doctors and nurses or to other factors, such as mothers' eating habits or drinking and drug taking?

Finally, there is also a distinction between higher and lower "levels" of induction. The fact that my computer has worked well for some time would normally be a good reason to think it will continue to work. But at some point, because we know from many other cases that computers eventually wear out, the fact that this one has worked for a long time begins to work *against* the belief it will continue to work. We know from looking at more cases over a longer term that this one, too, will eventually wear out. That higher level of inductive generalization allows a more refined judgment about an individual case. So, again, we see that probability theory and statistics are important to anyone who wants to do inductive reasoning well.

Some speculate that human beings use induction instinctively. Induction may well have even an evolutionary basis, since our ancestors who relied on it presumably lived to reproduce others who, like themselves, were good at induction while those who were not so good also were not successful at reproduction. Learning to recognize and run from dangerous animals meant they lived to produce offspring with the same talent. Whatever induction's origins, it's hard to imagine humans surviving long, let alone prospering, without the ability to learn from past experience and to generalize from that experience about what will happen in the future.

INFORMAL FALLACIES

*t*here are two ways to look at arguments from a logical point of view. You can study them formally, to see if they are strong (if inductive) or valid (if deductive). I've said a little about induction and will have more to say about deductive logic shortly. Another way to study arguments, besides looking to see if they follow good statistical or other formal rules, is to look at some of the ways reasoning typically goes off the tracks. The name given by logicians to the mistakes in reasoning we typically make is *fallacies*. Although there are probably about as many fallacies as there are people who reason, there are some forms of bad arguments to which human beings are especially vulnerable. These are the subject of this section.

The point of studying fallacies is similar to why it is useful to think about the nature of arguments and probability theory. By paying close attention to language and good reasoning patterns, we can become better reasoners.

Fallacies can be divided into groups. Sometimes the premises, even if true, do not support the conclusion. The premise may be either completely irrelevant to the truth of the conclusion, or though relevant there still may be a crucial "gap" between the premises and the conclusion that makes believing the conclusion unreasonable given the premises. Other times the argument is unacceptable for other reasons. As you read through the different types of fallacies, think about why they are fallacies but also about when an argument similar to that one might not be bad or fallacious.

Ad Hominem

Ad hominem means "to the person" or, literally, "to the man." The fallacy of ad hominem takes place when, instead of attacking a person's position or argument, the arguer instead attacks the *person* on irrelevant grounds. This fallacy often involves questioning a person's past activities or associations or needlessly referring to the person's background or interests. Sometimes such appeals carry great emotional feeling, but unless the personal trait is somehow relevant to the argument being offered, an ad hominem attack is not relevant to the conclusion. An obvious and therefore not very persuasive example is this: "Clinton's personal moral behavior was despicable, so his welfare reform proposals, which punish people who don't work, couldn't possibly make sense."

Appeal to Ignorance

This fallacy occurs because we often assume that since somebody has not proven that something is true, it must not be false (or vice versa). This is a common mistake. The fact that you cannot prove God exists does not mean God doesn't exist, just as the fact that we have not found out all the details of how evolution works does not show that the theory itself is false. But that said, it *is* often interesting and controversial just when it is a fallacy to appeal to ignorance. Sometimes the fact that something has not been proven true *should* be regarded as evidence against it. The fact that a good mechanic has gone over the car with a fine-toothed comb and found nothing is, presumably, good evidence the car is safe to buy. But the fact that we don't know exactly how cancer is caused by some chemical is not good evidence that the chemical is not the cause. It might be the cause and we just haven't figured out how it works yet.

Appeal to the People

This fallacy can take many forms, but the basic idea is that the arguer fallaciously appeals to the popularity of an idea or of an attitude as a justification. "All my friends are doing it" is a child's version, but adults are also often tempted to believe what others believe even when that popularity is insufficient to justify the belief. Bandwagon effects are what we sometimes call it, and they are common. It is also interesting in this connection that even voting and majority rule are not so much methods to establish a truth as a decision procedure that is accepted because it is fair. The truth about the world is not decided by a vote.

Appeal to Force

This fallacy occurs because the premise—that somebody is powerful—does not warrant the conclusion that the person is right or that the belief is correct. "Your money or your life" may give a good practical reason to turn over your wallet, but it is not a good reason for concluding you should do it. "If you don't go to class, you will fail" is again a good reason in the prudential sense, but it does not justify the professor's reasonableness in making the student attend.

Straw Man

Here the argument is fallacious because the arguer is attacking a position that is not, in fact, the one that the opponent is defending. Thus the attack is irrelevant. The author has in effect created a weaker, straw figure and merely attacked *it,* leaving untouched the original argument that was supposedly being criticized. Sometimes people think they have found a mistake in another's argument when, in fact, they have not interpreted it correctly—that is, they have not given the author the benefit of the doubt, or they have overlooked a more reasonable interpretation that does not involve the author in a mistake. So the straw man fallacy and the principle of charity are, in that sense, related: people who commit the fallacy are often not being charitable in interpreting what others mean. This is a pretty common fallacy, though identifying actual cases is not always easy and it may be controversial whether there really is a straw man. Sometimes people do give bad arguments after all.

Overgeneralization and Susceptibility to Counterexamples

Everybody generalizes when they think and write, and sometimes it's perfectly acceptable. But careful reasoners avoid reaching conclusions based on small samples or stereotypes. Some generalizations are "empirical"—that is, they are about the world and how it works. Others are about language, ideas, rules, and other standards. It's probably safe to say, based on what we know about their struggles, "The British people supported the Allied effort in World War II." However, if an author says that "U.S. youth hated the Vietnam war," there should be some pretty strong reasons to justify such a generalization. The same is true of statements like "Philosophers are skeptical about the objectivity of morality" and "Welfare recipients don't want to work." While such statements are undoubtedly sometimes true in individual cases, it's dangerous to make such sweeping claims without good evidence.

There are different ways to question a generalization. If the generalization is thought to apply without any exceptions, one *counterexample* can serve as a refutation. (There is a famous case in which a philosopher was giving a formal talk at the meeting of the American Philosophical Association. He told his audience that while it is common in English to use a double negative to mean a positive—it is "not unlikely," for instance—you never hear a double positive used as a negative. Another philosopher in the audience then yelled out, "Yeah, yeah.") We often use counterexamples to attack conceptual and moral claims. If it is suggested, for instance, that only rational human beings can have rights, you might suggest the counterexample of infants or perhaps even of Mr. Spock. (If a philosophical generalization is conceptual, as this one about rights seems to be, then it can be useful to think up imaginary cases as well as real ones.) Or suppose a theorist claimed that all laws are rules or that all rules are general commands. Thinking up a counterexample to a generalization would be one of the most familiar ways to dispute it. If the generalization is only that—a generalization—and is not meant to be universally true, then of course merely finding one counterexample does not refute it.

Gamblers' Fallacies

These fallacies are similar to overgeneralizations. While common among gamblers, they are also found in business and everyday life. One is the familiar idea that, once having lost the bet the last five times in a row, "my number has got to come up next time." The problem, of course, is that whether the number comes up next time is causally and statistically independent of what happened in the past. Flipping a coin still has a 50/50 chance of being heads, whatever it's been in the last few (or few hundred) tosses. Whether your car will make it to California may not, however, be independent of how it has been doing the past year. So whether or not the future is able to be predicted from past experience is itself a question that needs further thought; you can't just assume things will be the same or that they will change. Another gamblers' fallacy involves the belief that if we increase our bet each time, then eventually we must win. This is not true, as you can see if you calculate what will happen if somebody starts out betting one dollar, then after losing the first time, bets two, then three, then four, and so forth. On the other hand, *doubling* your bet after each loss will eventually ensure that you win (as long as you don't run out of money!).

Throwing Good Money (or Time) After Bad

Here's another favorite of mine, sometimes referred to as the "fallacy of sunk costs." Suppose you have already spent five dollars on a ticket but have since learned the movie is no good and you will probably not enjoy it. Many people will say, "I already spent the money, so I might as well just go." But that's a mistake. If you would rather do something else, such as going to a different movie, you should not compound your loss and pass up something you prefer just because you have made a mistake. It's better to admit the mistake and do something you would actually enjoy. This same idea—that we have something invested and so we should stick with it—can also occur in other contexts, for example, when we have spent time on a project. It applies to students too. If you have written a draft of a paper that has not panned out, don't think you must keep it. Sometimes it's best to start again. On the other hand, sometimes you can save even a bad paper by showing that what seemed a plausible idea didn't work out. Blind alleys are sometimes worth writing about after all.

Questionable Analogy

Arguing by analogy involves asserting that because two objects, situations, or events are similar in certain respects, the two must therefore share a further characteristic. Bad analogies are uncovered by pointing out that the two things are not in fact alike in the relevant ways, or that even if they were alike, that doesn't prove they share the further property. One famous example of analogical arguing (though it is much debated whether it is a fallacious analogy) involves a person who was kidnapped and hooked up for nine months to a violinist who needed her kidneys. The author, Judith Jarvis Thomson, used the analogy to show that because the violinist has no right to use the person's kidneys, an unborn baby has no right to use a mother's body either and so the mother can get an abortion.

Inconsistency

People are often inconsistent in some way, holding onto a premise or conclusion in one context that is incompatible with ones accepted in a different context. (This is a fallacy involving mistaken premises because inconsistent premises cannot both be true. Something has to give.) Rarely are people clearly and obviously inconsistent; however, in a more subtle way, it's always a danger. We may say something in one context, when writing about one issue, that we would not be willing to say in another, not having thought about the latter context. Or we may use a term in a subtly different sense in an argument, making the argument appear stronger than it is. This leads to the next category.

Equivocation and Ambiguity

Sometimes an argument depends on the author's equivocation between two different senses or meanings of a word or phrase, but you should reject the argument, because a key term or concept is used in one way in one context but another way elsewhere, thereby making a key premise false. To use a simple example, you should not accept the following argument: "People who own banks are probably quite wealthy, and Sue owns the bank next to her river, so Sue is probably wealthy." Other examples are not so silly; people often confuse themselves and others with imprecise words used different ways in different contexts. You can imagine, for example, that a person might accept the idea that lung cancer kills people and that smoking causes lung cancer yet not know or appreciate sufficiently how smoking kills.

Begging the Question

This fallacy occurs when, instead of giving a reason that establishes the conclusion, the conclusion is simply assumed. It is a fallacy because having assumed the (doubtful) conclusion as a premise, the arguer has not given a good reason to accept the conclusion. Often this occurs when a writer uses words that, on careful inspection, merely assert in different terms what's supposed to be proven. Here's an example: "God exists, because the Bible says so. And the Bible must be true, since it's the word of God." You can sometimes tell when a paper has made that mistake if a critic who reads it can reasonably say "Well, of course, if I accepted *that* as a premise, then I'd have to agree with you. But that premise is just another way of stating what you want to prove. And so you haven't proved anything." Politicians and political writers are especially prone to this fallacy when they evade or don't answer a question. In doing so, they assume what is at issue and so are guilty of begging the question. The fallacy also can occur in a longer argument chain, because of the distance between the premises and the conclusion, or where people ignore crucial but controversial or even very doubtful premises and simply assume they are true.

The phrase "begging the question" has come into popular usage recently, but it means something different. Sometimes people will say that someone "begs the question of . . ." and mean only that they have "raised the question of . . ." I have heard logicians get upset with that usage, claiming it is not the right way to think about begging the question. But since words' meaning can change, there may be little point in complaining. Still, I do agree that the logician's use of the term, the fallacy of begging the question, is an important idea to keep in mind.

Slippery Slope

This is just what it sounds like. Slippery slope arguments assume that if we take a first step, or two, then we will inevitably be led down a slippery slope to someplace we don't want to go. Because we reject the end point, it is claimed, we must therefore reject the beginning. This "slope" can be either logical or practical. It could be logical if the idea is that anybody accepting some argument would then logically have to accept a further, obviously unacceptable conclusion as well. Or you might think that were we to follow this advice, we'd be led down a path that would have disastrous practical or policy consequences. Sometimes slippery slope arguments are good, but often they are fallacies because the author simply assumes, without justification, that the first step will lead down the slope. To assess such arguments, think carefully about whether, and why, the first step will supposedly lead to the next and the next. If you unreasonably *assume* it does, you are guilty of the fallacy.

False Dilemma

In this case, the fallacious arguer unreasonably reduces the alternatives by arguing, for instance, that there are only two possibilities when, in fact, there are others. You can criticize a false dilemma most easily by pointing out the missed alternative, that is, by showing that it really is a dilemma. Sometimes it is assumed, for example, either that God exists and is the author of the moral law or that morality does not exist and everything is permitted. But there are alternative justifications of morality, besides divine commands, which shows that (at least without further evidence) this is a false dilemma.

Another example might be those who assume that human free will is a myth or else that our choices and decisions are uncaused. It could be argued that this is a false dilemma, since we could be free and at the same time all of our actions could be caused by prior events.

Red Herring

This fallacy gets its name from the fact that red herring fish were used to throw dogs off the scent when they were trying to track a person. The fallacy occurs when the arguer diverts attention away from the real issues to an irrelevant side issue. It differs from the straw man fallacy because there the opponent's argument is misinterpreted while in red herring the arguer changes the subject, ignoring the opponent's argument altogether.

False Accusation of a Fallacy

It's frequently controversial whether or not a fallacy is really present, so sometimes people even add "false accusation of a fallacy" to the list of fallacies. Be sure, therefore, to think about the possibility that *you* may have committed the mistake of falsely accusing the writer of committing a fallacy. Maybe the slippery slope fallacy is not a fallacy in this case, and the slope really is slippery? Or maybe your claim to have identified a doubtful analogy or straw man can itself be questioned?

It is critical, both in assessing and in giving an argument, to pay close attention to the various fallacies that might be committed. There are many types, and the ones mentioned above are only the most common. Finally, here's a very helpful exercise. Take the list of fallacies I have given, and go through a newspaper or magazine to see if you can find examples of the fallacies. Or, listen to some advertisements or to a political debate. Write down the argument (the premises and conclusion) being presented, and then ask yourself which, if any, of the fallacies I have described is being committed here. Doing that will make you a better reasoner and therefore a better student.

DEDUCTIVE LOGIC

*f*allacies of the sort we have been discussing are sometimes thought of as "informal" logic, as opposed to "formal." *Formal logic* gets its name because the correctness or incorrectness of the argument can be identified by the form of the argument alone. Informal fallacies don't work that way. There the mistake is not formal but depends instead on the specific content or meaning of the premises and conclusion, whether or not language is used ambiguously, whether irrelevant appeals are made to force and ignorance, and so on.

In this last section, I want to discuss briefly some of the central themes in formal, deductive logic. As I said above, it is concerned with argument forms alone, not their particular content. To see what that means, notice that different statements, while they mean something different, can have the same logical form. "Some doctors are males" and "Some horses are brown," for instance, have the same logical form. So do "Professors are teachers" and "Cats are mammals."

Validity and Soundness

A *valid* deductive argument is one whose premises, if true, establish the conclusion with certainty. It is impossible, in other words, for the premises to be true and the conclusion false. Sometimes it is obvious whether an argument form is valid. For example, it's clear that the following is formally valid. We don't need to know what A and B mean to know that if the premises are true, then the conclusion must also be true.

> Premise 1: If A then B (for example: If Sam is a cat, then Sam has a lung).
> Premise 2: A (Sam is a cat.)
> Therefore: B (Sam has a lung.)

It's also obvious that the following similar argument form is not valid, because there are plenty of instances where the premises are true but the conclusion is false.

> Premise 1: If A then B.
> Premise 2: B
> Therefore: A

If A stands for "Sam is a cat" and B for "Sam has lungs," then both the premise and the conclusion are true, but because Sam is in fact a dog, the conclusion is false. That single example shows the argument is not formally valid, even though many other examples exist in which the premises are true and the conclusion is also true.

Some arguments are less obviously either valid or invalid, and showing which is a complex problem. As discussed earlier in the chapter, there are also argument "chains," in which premises establish a conclusion but then that conclusion in turn provides premises for more arguments that eventually lead to the ultimate conclusion. Formal logic is concerned with seeing if there is a valid route to a conclusion from a given set of premises.

It is also sometimes tricky to distinguish deductive from inductive arguments. Recall that inductive arguments do not establish their conclusions with certainty; they only show the conclusion is more likely true, given that the premises are true. Even the fact that an argument uses "most" or "some" is not *necessarily* an indication that it is inductive. Consider the following argument.

Premise 1: Most doctors are wealthy.

Premise 2: Most doctors are conservative.

Conclusion: At least one doctor is wealthy and conservative.

This argument has the following form.

Premise 1: Most As are Bs.

Premise 2: Most As are C.

Conclusion: At least one A is both B and C.

Despite using "most," a term usually found in inductive arguments, this is a deductively valid argument because the premises, if true, establish the conclusion with certainty—that is, it is impossible for the premises to be true and the conclusion false. An invalid deductive argument would therefore be one in which it is claimed that the premises establish the conclusion with certainty, but they do not. (It should be clear from what's been said that the common idea that induction involves going from the particular to the general and that deduction involves going from the general to the particular is mistaken. Though some forms of inductive inferences do that, others don't. And though it is sometimes true that deductive arguments go from the general to the specific, it is not always so. "All men are mortal and no mortals are supernatural; therefore, no men are supernatural" is a valid deductive argument.)

It is also the case that any of the valid forms can have false premises and a false conclusion and still remain valid. For example, the following argument is valid even though its conclusion is not, in fact, true.

Premise 1: If a candidate won the popular vote, he won the presidency.

Premise 2: Al Gore won the popular vote.

Conclusion: Al Gore won the presidency.

What's wrong with the argument is not that it is in invalid, but that at least one of its premises is not true. *If* it were the case that candidates who win the popular vote win the presidency, then Gore would, indeed, be president. The problem is therefore not with the logic; it's not that there is a "gap" between the premises and the conclusion. Rather, the problem is that one of the premises is false. Logicians refer to it as deductively valid, but *unsound*, to indicate that distinction.

The reverse is also true: you can have an invalid deductive argument form with true premises and a true conclusion. Here is another example.

Premise 1: If it had rained, then the streets would be wet.

Premise 2: It didn't rain.

Conclusion: The streets are not wet.

This argument has this form:

Premise 1: If R then W.

Premise 2: Not R

Conclusion: Not W

But this is not a valid argument form, even if—as in the interpretation of it involving streets and rain—the conclusion and the two premises are all true. (For example, a fire hydrant could have been on.) Or consider the following argument with the same form.

Premise 1: If Felix is a dog, then Felix has lungs.

Premise 2: Felix is not a dog.

Conclusion: Felix does not have lungs.

If Felix is a cat, then although each of the premises is true (if Felix were a dog, he'd have lungs, and Felix is not a dog), we cannot therefore conclude that Felix does not have lungs since Felix is a cat.

Categorical Statements and the Square of Opposition

It is useful to begin studying deductive logic with the four classic forms of categorical statements, which express the logical relations among classes or groups of things. That is why they are unsurprisingly termed "categorical" statements. Imagine that As are any class or category of things whatsoever, from horses, people, or red herrings to sunny days, electrons, or things on your desk. Let's also assume that Bs are another class. Also assume that the term "some" means at least one, though it could include more than one. There are four categorical statements, with the traditional letter-names of A, E, I, and O.

All As are Bs (called form A).

No As are Bs (form E).

Some A is a B (form I).

Some A is not a B (form O).

These can each be put into diagram form by imagining circles or Venn diagrams in which shading indicates there is nothing there; a capital A or B refers to the particular class of things; and a lowercase x refers to an individual member of the class that exists. Here is how the four are diagramed.

(A) All As are Bs. (For example: *All apples are fruits.*)

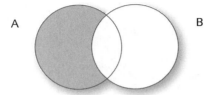

(E) No As are Bs. (*No apples are pears.*)

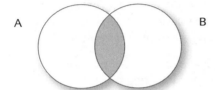

(I) Some A is a B. (*Some apples are red.*)

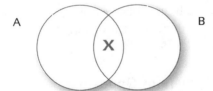

(O) Some A is not a B. (*Some apples are not red.*)

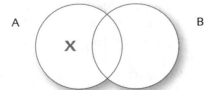

The differences between these four can be expressed in terms of their *quality* and *quantity.* Quality asks whether the statement affirms or negates class membership. So A and I are affirmative in quality, while E and O are negative. Quantity asks whether the statement says something about every member of the subject class. (The "subject class is the As in the examples, and the "predicate" class is the Bs.) Statements A and E are universal, because they do make a claim about the entire subject class, while I and O forms are particular, since they claim something about only some members of A. This can be summarized as follows.

A form is universal affirmative.

E is universal negative.

I is particular affirmative.

O is particular negative.

Notice, too, that you can draw many different logical conclusions even from these single statement forms depending on whether they are true or false. So, for instance, if we assume the A form (All As are Bs) is true, then "Some As are Bs" is also true, "No As are Bs" is false, and "Some As are not Bs" is false. Similarly, we can ask about the truth of the others if "All As are Bs" is false rather than true, and we can do the same for the three other statements, asking what, if anything, we can know about the others if that logical form is assumed to be true or false.

These relationships are expressed in terms of contradiction, contraries, subcontraries, and subalterns. In general, two statements are the *contradictories* of each other if they must have the opposite "truth value," that is, when they cannot both be either true or false. They are *contraries,* on the other hand, when they cannot both be true but can be anything else. *Subcontraries* cannot both be false but can be anything else. Finally, *subalterns* occur when one statement's being true requires that a second be true, while the second statement's being false means the first must be false. So "All A is B" and "Some A is B" are subalterns. If the universal is true, then so is the particular. If the particular is false, on the other hand, then so is the universal. "No A is B" and "Some A is not B" are also subalterns.

These relationships are summarized in what is called the *traditional square of opposition,* as follows.

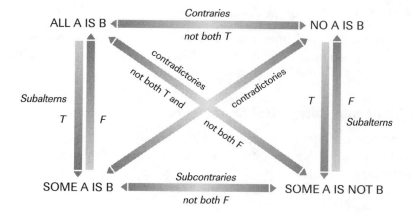

Conversion, Contraposition, and Obversion

But that's not all. Suppose we agree that "non-A" refers to the *complement* of the class of As, by which we mean everything that is not an A. That would mean that if we combined the classes of both A and non-A, we would have included everything that exists, in other words. But now notice that we can use this idea of the complement of a class of things to draw even more inferences from the A, E, I, and O forms.

Conversion means simply switching the A and the B (subject and predicate) terms, so that the converse of "All A is B" is "All B is A," of "No A is B" is "No B is A," and so forth. Notice, then, that the converse of the E and the I forms have the same truth value but that others do not. In other words, if "Some A is B" is true (or false), then "Some B is A" is true (or false). The same goes for the I form. But the A form and its converse, "All As are Bs" and "All Bs are As," do not have the same truth value, nor does the O and its converse, "Some As are not Bs" and "Some Bs are not As."

Contraposition is just like conversion except that when you switch the A and B terms, you also replace each of them with its complement. For instance, "All A is B" has as its contrapositive "All non-B is non-A." Contrapositives are equivalent for the two forms that are not equivalent for conversion, that is, for the A and O forms.

Last but not least is *obversion,* which works for all four forms. To get the obverse of one of the four statement forms, you simply change the quality, from negative to positive or vice versa, and then substitute the complement for the second class (B). Here are the obverses of each of the four forms.

All A is B. = No A is non-B.

No A is B. = All A is non-B.

Some A is B. = Some A is not non-B.

Some A is not B. = Some A is non-B.

So, for instance, if "All horses are mammals" is true, then "No horses are nonmammals" is true; if "No horses are brown" is false, then "All horses are nonbrown" is also false, and so on.

Translating into Categorical Statements

The examples of statements I have given so far all clearly resemble the A, E, I, or O form. But with a little imagination, other statements with apparently different forms can also be put into the categorical form, showing that what they mean either asserts or denies membership in classes. To do that, we must sometimes introduce a new term—people, times, things—that reflects the class or category the statement refers to. For example, "Smokers run the risk of getting sick" can be translated as "All smokers are people who risk getting sick." Similarly, "Dogs bark" could be correctly translated as "All dogs are things that bark" or its converse, "No dogs are things that do not bark." Or "Students never walk to school" can be put into the form "No times are times students walk to school" or "No students are beings that walk to school." Here are some other examples of translations. (Paying attention to how to translate ordinary statements into categorical ones is an excellent way to become more attuned to the meanings of the words we use, and also to their misuse.)

Every jet in our fleet is safe. = All jets in our fleet are things that are safe.

Somebody should get out here fast. = Some persons are persons who should get out here fast.

Any believer in God is religious. = All people who believe in God are religious.

Only an idealist would vote for him. = All persons who would vote for him are idealists. (Or we could use the obverse: No persons who would vote for him are nonidealists.)

I eat anything that is put before me. = All things put before me are things I eat. (Notice that this is not the same as its converse.)

Nobody who eats this will enjoy it. = No person who eats this is a person who will enjoy it.

Whatever I do is wrong. = All things I do are things that are wrong.

Sometimes we have to sacrifice ourselves for the greater good. = Some times are times we have to sacrifice ourselves for the greater good.

Whoever loved the novel will hate the movie. = All people who loved the novel are people who will hate the movie. (Notice you could also say: No person who loved the novel is a person who will not hate the movie. Can you name the second translation?)

Raising taxes will make some people very unhappy. = All times we raise taxes are times we will make some people very unhappy.

"Only" and "none but" are easily confused. For instance, "Only the deserving will get the prize" means "All persons who get the prize are deserving."

Don't confuse the classes here; it's easy to do. "The only" and "only" can also be confused. For instance:

> The only dogs that are smart are labs. = All smart dogs are labs. (Not: All labs are smart dogs.)

"Except" and "but" generally require *two* statements. For example:

> Everyone except (or but) my enemies are coming to my party. = No enemies of mine are coming to my party *and* "All persons who are not my enemies are persons who are coming to my party."

Take a moment to think about why both of these statements are required to express the statement.

We can also identify the logical form of statements about individual things. These seem to be neither universal statements about classes nor particular statements of the I and O forms. It is, however, possible to translate them into the A form. Suppose we want to say something about a fine steed named Trigger, maybe something imaginative like "Trigger is a horse." One option is to imagine a class with only one member in it, Trigger, and turn it into a categorical A form. So we could say "All T (where T refers to the class with one member, Trigger, in it) is a horse."

But we can also diagram it this way, assuming "t" refers to the individual horse Trigger.

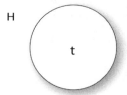

And then we can put it into this argument.

> Premise 1: All horses have hooves.
>
> Premise 2: Trigger is a horse.
>
> Conclusion: Trigger has hooves.

This argument is about a class of things, horses, and one individual thing, Trigger. It is also logically valid—if the premises are true, then the conclusion must also be true—because of its form alone. We can see this by imagining that we are not speaking just of horses but of any class of things, and not just of Trigger but of any individual thing. Looked at that way, the form of the argument, which is what makes it valid, is this.

Premise 1: All Ps are Qs.

Premise 2: t is a P.

Conclusion: t is Q.

Diagramming and Testing Arguments

So it's clear why we say that a logical form is valid, meaning that whatever you substitute for the form, the argument is still valid. All other arguments of the same form as the one about Trigger—such as "All professors are handsome, Arthur is a professor, so Arthur is handsome"—are also deductively valid (assuming "handsome" refers here to the class of handsome people). *If* those two premises are (were) true, then it would indeed follow logically that Arthur is handsome. But of course, if the premises are (were) not true, then alas the conclusion is not (necessarily) true either—though it might be!

Because deductive validity is a formal idea and does not depend on the specific classes or individuals referred to in the argument for it to be valid, there are many forms of valid deductive arguments. And since validity means that if the premises are true then the conclusion *must* also be true, it follows that the conclusion is in a sense "included" in the premises. You can show this by using the diagramming technique I described. If you have three classes, you can represent them with three interlocking circles, like this.

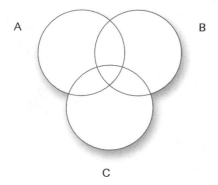

If you diagram each of the premises, then you will not have to change or add to the diagram for the conclusion to be represented in the diagram. That shows the argument is valid. Here, then, is the diagram of the following argument.

Premise 1: All As are Bs.

Premise 2: All Bs are Cs.

Conclusion: All As are Cs.

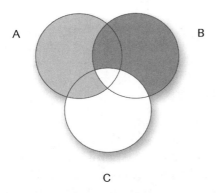

As you can see, though I only diagrammed the two premises, doing so also diagrammed the conclusion.

Here is a diagram of another valid argument, using a particular as well as universal statement forms. (You should always diagram the universal statements first, by doing the shading, then put in the Xs to represent the particular statement forms.)

Premise 1: All A is B.

Premise 2: Some A is not C.

Conclusion: Some A is B.

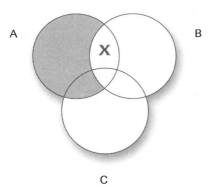

Finally, here is the diagram showing the validity of the argument involving Trigger. I am using a small t to represent Trigger and an H to represent the class of horses. (Again, be sure to do your shading first, before putting in statements about individuals or members of classes.)

Premise 1: All Hs are Qs.

Premise 2: t is a H.

Conclusion: t is Q.

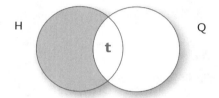

(For fun, try translating the argument about Trigger into an argument using only the A form and then testing it for validity.)

Disjunctive and Conditional Statements

The square of opposition, the three relations I just described (conversion, obversion, and contraposition), and the arguments we have diagrammed all draw inferences using classes and can be put into one of the four standard categorical propositions. Two other statement forms are especially noteworthy, however, and they too have their own names. One is the *disjunctive* form: for instance, "Either you will give me your money, or I will shoot you" and "Either it will rain, or we will have the picnic outside." The disjunctive form is "P or Q." It does not assert either P or Q but, instead, that at least one or the other is true. A second form of statement is called the *conditional:* for instance, "If you do not stop, then I will refuse to go out with you again." This has the logical form of "If P then Q."

Sometimes the conditional form can be put into a categorical proposition and the argument tested for validity. For instance, we could translate "If it is sunny, then I will go along" as "All times that it is sunny are times I will go along." (Obviously, the obverse and contrapositive are equivalent, but might that statement, depending on context, also mean the converse?) Some conditional statements cannot be translated into the A, E, I, or O forms, however—for instance, "If my new house is in Binghamton, then my first house is in San Jose."

Notice too that conditional statements are very common in ordinary speech. "Unless," for instance, generally means "if . . . not." For instance, "I will go with you unless you are rude" means "If you are rude, I won't go with you." That, in turn, can be translated as "All times you are rude are times I won't go with you." Similarly, "We will go swimming unless it rains" can be translated as "All times we go swimming are times it does not rain" or as "No times we go swimming are times it rains"—that is, the obverse of the first translation.

These conditional and hypothetical statement forms can also, of course, be part of arguments, and those arguments can be either valid or invalid. Here are some examples of obviously valid argument forms using the disjunctive and conditional statement forms that we have already met.

Premise 1: If P then Q.

Premise 2: P

Conclusion: Q

(This even has its own name. It is called *modus ponens.*)

Premise 1: If P then Q.

Premise 2: Not Q

Conclusion: Not P

(This is traditionally called *modus tollens.*)

Premise 1: P or Q

Premise 2: Not Q

Conclusion: P

Each of these is deductively valid, which means that any premises of that form, if true, establish the truth of any conclusion of that form. Arguments with disjunctive statements often cannot be shown to be valid using the categorical logic we have been discussing, because the translation does not adequately express the meaning of the disjunction. (For example, we can translate "It will rain or it will snow" as "All times are times it will rain or snow," but doing that does not allow us to test the argument's validity.)

Here is an example of an *invalid* argument in categorical form. Can you prove it is invalid by diagramming it? (Remember, if it is invalid, then diagramming the premises will not also diagram the conclusion.)

Premise 1: No As are Bs.

Premise 2: No Bs are Cs.

Conclusion: No As are Cs.

Now see if you can give an interpretation of it—that is, find specific classes to substitute for the A, B, and C where the premises are obviously true and the conclusion is false. This is one way to prove any argument is invalid. If you can think up an interpretation of it in which the premises are true but the conclusion is false, then you have shown the argument to be invalid. (Try horses, cars, and mammals for the above argument if you are stuck.) In fact, we often reason that way. We say things like "If yours were a good argument, then this conclusion would have to follow from these premises. . . . But obviously we know that's not right, so we know that your argument doesn't work." That is just one of the many uses of logic. If you fail to think up a case showing that the premises can be true and the conclusion false, it does not follow that the argument is invalid. It might be, perhaps you just haven't yet thought up an interpretation that proves it is invalid.

I've tried in this section to give you a brief taste of what logic is about by emphasizing categorical logic.[2] In fact, logic as a field has long surpassed the approach we have been discussing. I do think, though, that this is a great way to begin to appreciate the value of logic. Studying logic encourages more care in reasoning as well as a greater appreciation for the nature of arguments, the complexities of language, and the importance of knowing what we, and others, mean. This leads us to the next subject: how to read and understand what you are reading.

Review Questions and Exercises

After you have completed your responses, refer to Appendix II to check your answers.

1. What is reasoning and why is reasoning important, according to the book? Do you agree? Explain.

2. Explain the meaning of each of the following terms:
   A. Statement
   B. Argument
   C. Premise and conclusion

3. Explain the difference between an inductive and a deductive argument. Name the four types of inductive arguments.

4. Find an editorial in a newspaper or magazine, and study it carefully. Is it giving an argument? If so, what is the argument? If there is more than one argument, or if there is an argument chain, explain that too.

5. Keep a notebook in which you cut out and explain examples of as many of the fallacies as you can find.

6. What is the difference between a particular statement and a statement form? Give an example.

---

[2]Here's a suggestion. Just for fun, return to the square of opposition and ask yourself what would happen if the argument you were considering, while using the A, E, I, and O form, were about either a class that has no members or individuals that do not exist. What would be the implications of that for the logical relationships in the square? Does the traditional square of opposition work only for classes with members, not for gremlins or individuals such as Hamlet and Santa Claus? But can we not say, truly, of Hamlet that he was the prince of Denmark and not of Sweden, and of Santa Claus that he wears red rather than pink? Logicians have thought—with great success—a great deal about how to deal with such problems. But you'll have to take a logic class to learn more.

7. Give examples of the four statement forms in the square of opposition.

8. Show how to diagram each of the four statement forms in the square of opposition.

9. What does it mean when two statements "contradict" each other? Which statements in the square of opposition are contradictories? Answer the same questions for contraries, subcontraries, and subalterns.

10. What is the "converse" of a statement? Give an example. When are these equivalent?

11. What is the "obverse" of a statement? Give an example. When are these equivalent?

12. What is the "contrapositive" of a statement? Give an example. When are these equivalent?

13. Put the following statements into one of the four categorical statement forms A, E, I, or O. (Remember, sometimes you may have to introduce words like "days" or "times" or even "things" in order to do the translation.)

    A. Women are emotionally stronger than men.
    B. Firefighters are never cowards.
    C. Everyone who buys a ticket wins a prize.
    D. If something is illegal, whoever does it is a criminal.
    E. Nobody who goes to that store should have a clear conscience.
    F. Some people who speak do so out of turn.
    G. Lovers are friends.
    H. Friends are not always lovers.
    I. Whoever is reading this is literate.
    J. Only a fool still supports Communism.
    K. Capitalists are all exploiters.
    L. Everybody who has met both Tom and Tim prefers Tom.
    M. Dracula loves to eat out.
    N. Thomas is neither mean nor angry.
    O. Everything that exists is made of matter.
    P. I will go to the beach unless it rains.
    Q. The only cats that are smart are tigers.
    R. None but the winners should be on the field.
    S. All except for students who failed the exam can leave.

14. Put each of these into categorical argument form, indicating the premise(s) and conclusion.

   A. Every poodle is a dog, and all dogs are mammals. So each poodle is a mammal.

   B. Some Communists were atheists, so some atheists were Communists.

   C. Nobody who works hard is a capitalist, so no president has been a capitalist since all presidents work hard.

   D. Whoever is a heavy drinker is a bad driver. Melissa never drinks, so she's not a bad driver.

15. Test the arguments in question 14 for validity, using a diagram.

16. Find a deductive argument in the media, then test it for validity.

how to read

AND UNDERSTAND WHAT YOU ARE READING

READ ACTIVELY AND CHARITABLY

Chapter 2 discussed two types of assignments: (1) those designed to provide facts and information and (2) those designed to teach students how to solve problems. This chapter concerns the third important category: reading persuasive essays. These can be as short as a few pages or as long as a book or even a whole series of books. The central idea behind this type of writing is to persuade you of something new or to change or modify your beliefs on an issue. Sometimes it will include new information, of course, which can be factual information, distinctions between different senses of words that help clarify a problem, or descriptions of subtle features of human experience that have gone unnoticed. But the larger point is to persuade.

This means, then, that you must read actively, keeping in mind the development of the essay. The place to begin is with the *conclusion* or *thesis:* what is the author trying to get you to believe or reject? The second part of the problem is to become clear on the reasoning or the ground that the author thinks supports the conclusion. If you can't understand *both what the author wants you to think and why,* you have not yet understood what you have read. You therefore have to think about it as you read, always asking what the author is trying to say, where the essay is headed, and how it is getting there.

If you are having trouble, read slowly; persuasive essays are not like reading a newspaper. Proceed to the next sentence only after you have a fairly good idea of what the one you're now reading means (or you're at least convinced that you can't possibly figure it out). This is especially true for people who have not had years of experience reading this type of essay, though in truth it applies to the rest of us as well.

A second difference between people who are good at reading and understanding and those who are not is that good readers are *charitable* readers. Your goal as a reader is to understand, to see how the world looks from the author's perspective. What is he or she trying to show, and why? If you are to appreciate and understand what you read, you cannot begin with the assumption that the author is foolish, prejudiced, or misguided. That may be true, of course; some authors are all those things. But assuming this gets the cart before the horse. Instead, assume that there is something here worth thinking about, something worthwhile to be gotten from the essay. If you don't do that, you will almost surely never really appreciate what you are reading and therefore never understand it.

This is very important and worth emphasizing. Often, students' and other readers' initial attitudes and biases interfere with their ability to understand what the author is saying. If you resist, criticize, or misinterpret, you will not understand. Successful readers learn to tame their own negative attitudes and to read charitably, looking for the wisdom and intelligence in whatever they are trying to understand. As I said, if you come to material with a negative attitude that presumes an author is wrong, misguided, or worse, you will almost surely not understand what is being said.

Of course, that is not to say you should accept everything you read: that would be foolish, even if it were possible. The point, rather, is to avoid dismissing material too quickly, before its meaning is clear. So I suggest the principle of charity: assume as you read that this author is a reasonable person trying to make sense of a difficult problem. You may begin, of course, as we all sometimes do, with a preconceived impression that nobody who takes a position like *that* could possibly be worth reading. If you are to understand fully what you read, however, you would be wise to reserve that judgment until you have heard, and fully understood, what the author has to say. Charity rules.

THREE STEPS TO UNDERSTANDING WHAT YOU READ

*t*his section provides some specific steps you can follow as you read assignments, steps that will enable you to understand what you have read and to increase your chances of being well prepared for class discussions, exams, and papers. Because understanding essays is sometimes difficult (that's what makes them so interesting!), you cannot just read through quickly. Instead, you have to think—and almost always write—as you go along. It is essential to underline or highlight as you read, noting key passages. It also helps to write notes in the margins. These notes can be comments and questions you have or brief phrases and sentences summarizing what the author is saying. As you read, look for summaries and overviews that the author gives. It is also good, after you've read, underlined, and annotated the text, to distill what you've read into a short synopsis in the form of an outline or brief essay. I often find that when I need to understand something well, there is nothing better than making a synopsis. The goal is to capture the core or essence of the assignment. Here, spelled out, are three steps to follow as you read.

Step 1. Get a Sense of the Big Picture

What should you do as you start out to read an essay or chapter of a book? First, try to get a general sense of the author's overall objective and approach: what is it you are supposed to believe or see that you don't already? Begin with the title: what does it tell you about the subject or the thesis the author is defending? Often you can also get a good idea of the general drift of the work from an editor's introduction, if there is one. It also helps to look briefly at the beginning of the piece and then to take a peek at the very end, where authors often summarize what they have tried to do. Ask yourself these questions: What issue, theory, or argument is being discussed here? What seems to be the main point? Is the author responding to somebody else's argument or making an entirely new contribution to the subject? Also, consider *why* you are reading the material in the course. Remember that the readings fit into a larger whole—the book or the course—and have been chosen because of their contribution to these larger problems or topics.

Once you have a general sense of the big picture, you can proceed to the next step, where you study more carefully and in detail the specific structure of the argument.

Step 2. Identify the Argument Structure

After you have a general feel for the essay's larger objectives and basic approach, go back and read it more closely, keeping in mind that you're using the principle of charity to find the author's conclusion or thesis and its supporting reasons. Are these key ideas stated explicitly, or do you have to guess on the basis of scattered comments? Is the author defending the conclusion directly, or trying to show that somebody else's argument is mistaken?

Next, focus on how the author reaches this conclusion. All persuasive arguments begin somewhere; they take certain ideas as given, not needing further proof. Those starting points, on which the conclusion is based, are the argument's premises or assumptions. If you accept them, it is claimed, then you should also accept the conclusion. There is nothing simple or uninteresting about the process of figuring out the premises and conclusion of an argument. Think of what you are studying as an *argument path,* keeping in mind that the author is claiming that you should accept the conclusion (follow this path) based on other beliefs you already hold or beliefs that it's reasonable to expect you to accept. Notice too that the author may be giving a series or chain of arguments, with one conclusion providing the premise for another argument, leading eventually to the final conclusion. If so, then you need to identify that chain as part of the structure.

In addition to watching for argument chains, keep an eye out for these different forms of argument. For instance, authors often appeal to a *general principle* that, it is claimed, establishes the conclusion the writer is defending. Or you may notice an *argument by analogy,* in which, for example, affirmative action might be defended by comparing society with a footrace in which everybody should have an equal chance to compete. Frequently an author will *criticize* positions of others, including perhaps your own, by giving reasons why the ideas other accept are mistaken. (See the discussion on reasoning and some typical types of fallacies in Chapter 4.)

Before you reject the essay you are reading as flawed, remember what I said earlier about the importance of being charitable as you read and of setting aside any hostility you feel in order to appreciate what is being claimed. Ask yourself why a thoughtful person might take this position by trying to see things through the author's eyes. In other words, don't let your disagreement with what you are reading cloud your ability to understand. Often you may find it difficult to see exactly how the essay is supposed to fit together or how some point is relevant to the larger issue. But you haven't really understood the essay until you have grasped this larger framework or structure.

One additional caveat: as I've said, authors often discuss and then criticize the views of others. It is very important, therefore, to keep from confusing times when the author is explaining or summarizing *somebody else's* ideas or argument with the times when the author is giving *his own* position. A historian, for instance, might first present the case that the bombing of Hiroshima was justified and then go on to explain why that argument fails. But readers frequently find this confusing because they overlooked a crucial sentence in which the author said something like "Consider the following argument" or "Johnson's position is that . . ." This practice of summarizing and explaining a position, only to have it be refuted later, can often seem very persuasive and can sometimes go on for pages. If you are to understand what you read, however, it is vital to know when the author is saying what other people believe, or might believe, and when it's the author's own ideas.

Clearly, then, it is not easy to understand fully a persuasive essay; a text must be read very carefully if you are to uncover its argumentative structure. It may also require interpretation on your part, since few writers are clear on every point. You may have to read the text slowly, line by line. Reading aloud can help, and taking notes as you read is almost always a must.

Step 3. Write a Synopsis Outline or Short Essay

Until you can outline or in some other way summarize the essay and explain it to yourself or someone else in your own words, you have not really understood the material. It may be tempting to skip this step because it seems so basic compared to evaluating and criticizing. You may also worry that other people have less trouble than you in simply understanding what's being said, and you may spend less time on it yourself. But that's wrong: professional researchers and professors spend a great deal of time trying to figure out the exact meaning of what they read. Often this is much more than half the battle: your evaluation of what you've read can be fairly easy to tease out once you fully understand what's being claimed and why.

The best way to test whether or not you understand what you have read is to try to give a synopsis of it. This can be in either of two forms: an outline or a short summarizing essay. The idea is to explain in your own words what the author is trying to say. Usually that means figuring out what the conclusion is—what you are supposed to think having read the essay—and the reasons the author has given in support of it. The old, familiar expression "I know what I want to say, but I just can't say it" is a fraud. *If you can't explain it, you don't understand it.* You may think you do, but you won't really know until you try to explain it. This is why people often say things like "You don't really understand something until you try to teach it." The point is the same: you might believe you know, but the proof is in the explaining or (in the case of math) in the doing.

Finally, if you really want to understand something, or to test your understanding, try giving a synopsis. You should begin with a sentence or two explaining the context: how does this reading fit into its larger context? (This is especially important if it is part of a larger book or essay.) Then try to explain the heart or essence of what you read. What, precisely, did the author want readers to come away believing? How did the author try to establish that conclusion? Was the point that somebody else was wrong, or did the author ignore other thinkers and simply argue for one position or another? If, as is usual, there was one master conclusion and other subsidiary ones along the way, which was which? Which of the subsidiary arguments were defended, and which ones were left undefended? What distinctions did the author make, and how did they support the larger point the author was trying to establish?

CRITICALLY EVALUATE WHAT YOU HAVE READ

Once you understand the central ideas being put forth—the general thesis and the reasons offered to support the thesis—the next step is to *evaluate* what you have read, trying to assess the essay's strengths and weaknesses. This assessment can take many forms and depends crucially on what the author has claimed and why. What you are basically asking is whether or not the author's basic contentions are true, and whether or not the author's reasons, offered in defense of the thesis, are good reasons.

There are about as many different issues here as there are essays: each one is unique in important ways. That means you can ask all kinds of questions about what you read, raising fresh objections to the author's generalizations, questioning analogies, and making new distinctions that clarify or even try to refute the thesis. Here are just a few of the kinds of questions to ask as you reflect critically on what you have read.

- Does some new information the author has provided really establish the thesis?

- Is a distinction that the author has made useful in establishing the conclusion? Is it a real distinction or merely a verbal one that does not indicate a genuine difference?

- Has the author assumed that some generalization is true when in fact you can think of counterexamples or instances in which the generalization does not hold?

- Is the author's criticism of another writer sound? What was that other writer really trying to say? Is it what this author said he said? Could the other writer be interpreted more charitably as not making that mistake? How might that writer respond to this author's criticisms?

Suppose you have thought about the ideas being presented and have discovered that the argument has problems, that you don't think it works? Perhaps the analogy on which it relies is faulty. Having said what you think is wrong, you may also want to ask whether—if you had been the author—you would have made any changes that would establish the conclusion on firmer ground. If you found a weakness in one of the author's assumptions, for example, ask yourself how the author's view could be defended against your objection and whether you would then find it acceptable.

The key, in short, is to think like a lawyer—or, rather, like *two* lawyers. Put yourself in the position of defending or criticizing a position; then imagine how your opponent would respond to what you or somebody else has just written. This process can be carried on in successive stages as you assess the essay, asking how the author might reasonably answer potential objections. One take-home lesson is that reading passively through the pages is never adequate; you've got to pay very close attention in order to identify the basic thesis of the essay and its general argumentative structure. Then, after you've done that, you need to go on to evaluate critically what you have read by searching out all the weaknesses that may be present in the essay. Keep in mind that slow reading, surprisingly, is generally more interesting than skimming. Think of it as an opportunity for a virtual conversation or a debate with a very smart person.

Review Questions and Exercises

1. What does it mean to read actively? To read charitably? Explain why each is important to understanding.

2. What specific steps can be taken at the beginning, before you read something, to help you understand better as you read?

3. Explain what an argument structure is.

how to do well on exams

PREPARING FOR THE EXAM

By the time you get to college, you've already had a fair amount of experience taking exams. Unfortunately, however, many students do less well on tests than they could, either because they didn't spend time wisely when preparing for the exam or because they made strategic mistakes while actually taking it. So here are some suggestions that I hope you will find useful when taking tests. Some of them will seem pretty obvious, so the question may be how to motivate yourself to do what you already know is the best way to study. Others, however, will not be so obvious.

First, keep in mind that no amount of last-minute effort can make up for failure to do your work throughout the semester. So much of what has been said in the previous chapters about taking notes on readings and during class goes double here. If you've done that, you're already more than halfway home. If, on the other hand, you haven't been doing your work right along, good luck. It's not too late to improve your grade, but you've made life a whole lot more difficult for yourself.

Begin studying well before exam day. Then, as the examination approaches, you should first try to learn all you can about the type of exam you will face. If your professor has taught this class before, try to get copies of old exams. Some professors make their old exams available to students, while some don't; pay close attention to the professor and to other students so you can learn as much as possible about the material to be covered and the format of the exam. You should definitely try to get certain questions resolved well in advance: will the exam have problems to solve, essay questions, short-answer questions, or a combination? Will it cover material from lectures exclusively, or will there also be material from the readings but not discussed in class? Will the essays be open ended, or will the professor be looking for specific answers? Will you be asked to go beyond what you have studied, to offer your own ideas?

After you've learned as much as you can about the exam, look over your notes, checking to see if you are missing some and whether you can recollect the class lectures and discussions as you read through the notes. Once you've gotten the notes in order, it's time to get serious. First, fill in the holes, getting missing notes from friends, if necessary. Different people devise their own strategies, but I think the best is to copy notes over—not word for word, but more clearly and succinctly. Think of it as *taking notes on your notes*. Sometimes good students do this more than once, so that what have begun as 100 pages of notes is distilled to 10 pages.

Depending on the nature of the exam, you may want to go back over the readings. Another useful study aid may be flashcards with questions on one side and answers on the other. This works well if you expect short-answer questions, definitions, and the like. It's also useful to outline or even sketch out complete answers to questions you think are likely to appear. Old examinations are very helpful here. Finally, if you took my earlier advice, you began studying well before the test and will not be forced to stay up late cramming the night before. Not only will you be more alert during the exam, but you'll also be more confident and less nervous if you've prepared early— all of which gives you a great advantage.

HINTS FOR TAKING DIFFERENT TYPES OF TESTS

*L*et's go back to the distinctions I made in Chapter 2 among different goals that professors have in making assignments. I said there are three main ones: (1) to convey information and facts, (2) to solve problems, and (3) to understand readings that present an argument or interpretation (persuasive essays). Examinations will reflect those same objectives and priorities.

When you get an exam, look it over before you start to write anything (except your name and other information). Then think about how much different parts of the exam will probably count toward the total grade, and make a rough schedule for yourself of how much time to spend on different parts. Timing is critical in many exams: you don't want to write so much on one question that you have insufficient time left for others. Most exams are structured so you do best if you get the core of the answer down for all of them rather than going into great detail on one question but leaving others unanswered.

Be sure, too, that you focus on the precise questions being asked. Again and again, professors come across answers that do not really answer the question directly and clearly but instead go on and on about related (or unrelated) issues. Usually, that time has been wasted. Answering two out of three questions fully and then writing a few rushed notes on the last one is almost always disastrous.

Here, then, is some specific advice about what to do when you're actually taking the test.

1. First, read the exam through, and make note of how much time you should spend on different parts.

2. If optional questions have been provided, decide which questions you will answer. Mark those questions, and double-check to see that you are answering the right number. Answering extra questions can sometimes be as bad as skipping questions.

3. Plan carefully how you will answer each question. Try to imagine the answer the professor is looking for on the question. Why was that question included on the test? Time spent analyzing the question is rarely wasted. This may well take you 5 or 10 minutes, by which time others may be scribbling away. Don't worry about that.

4. Do not make the common mistake of imagining that you can impress the professor by writing down everything you know. Often, the best answers are the briefest, and you may need the time to answer other questions.

5. If you finish early, reread each question and answer. You may find you've misinterpreted a question, and you almost certainly will find a way to make your ideas (or your penmanship) a bit clearer.

6. Write neatly, or print if you must. You'd be surprised how often professors have trouble understanding an answer because the writing is hard to decipher.

In sum: *Think about each of the questions before you write, manage your time carefully, and keep your cool.*

Review Questions and Exercises

1. What steps should be taken in preparing for an examination?
2. When you are taking an examination, describe the best way to proceed.

how to write a good paper

GETTING STARTED

"Where do I start?" is a familiar question from students who stand at the precipice, ready to begin writing, but who haven't a clue what to do next. The best place to begin is by asking what the professor has in mind when assigning a paper or essay. There is no single answer. Some papers emphasize research, gathering information and then distilling it into a discussion of a specific idea or theme. Other papers emphasize the development of your own critical ideas. In this case, the goal is to defend a position by giving reasons; you stake out a claim, and then argue for it. This occurs in many areas, from history and political science to literature and art. So you will need to think for a few minutes, at least, about the kind of paper this is supposed to be. Are you supposed to develop a thesis and argue for it, for instance, or only to report on research you do?

By the time you write your first paper for your class, you should have a sense from the readings and the professor's lectures or discussions the approach you should take. But if you don't, by all means ask. Some professors may assign a specific topic, while others might give students the option of choosing their own (more on that in a moment).

Because writing a paper usually involves explaining and, ultimately, assessing what you have read elsewhere, you must understand the material you plan to discuss in order to write about it (which takes us back to the earlier discussions of preparing for class and understanding what you are reading). But, alas, reading up on the subject and understanding what you have read are only the first steps.

It also helps to remember—and this is very important—that you don't have to have everything clear in your mind before starting to write. Writing is virtually never like that, though sometimes people who haven't written a lot imagine that it is. Writers don't first think and think and then, only after they know precisely what they want to say, sit down and put it on paper. Instead, it is *through* the process of writing that you discover and clarify what you want to say. You may also find that what you wanted to say initially was hopelessly confused, not worth saying, or just plain wrong. So keep in mind as you start that the familiar model of first thinking about what you want to write and then putting it all down is wrong. Writing *is* thinking. You need to have some sense of the subject and approach you plan to take, of course, but that's a far cry from having everything worked out in advance.

Second, don't get discouraged. Remember that writing a paper is typically a mixture of everything from frustrating absence of progress to slow progress to sudden inspiration. If you're not sure what you want to say, you can always begin by describing somebody else's article or an argument that you found interesting.

I suggest either of two ways to get started: the *just do it* way and the *organized* way. The "just do it" approach is just that. Think of it as brainstorming in order to get yourself started. After you have done the basic reading and note taking, just start writing on some topic, keeping in mind that nothing you say can be used against you. It can always be erased. The idea with the "just do it" approach is to suspend critical faculties by writing down as quickly as possible whatever comes into your head. It does not have to be in any logical order, nor should you bother to correct spelling and grammatical errors or question whether you have evidence for what you assert. For many students, a computer is a great aid to producing such a splurge because what has been written seems to be only a flickering commitment that can be revised or deleted. Once completed, the pages can be printed out and used as the beginning of a more thorough, careful discussion of the issues. Another helpful way to get started, if you don't yet have any idea of what you want to say, is to write summaries of what others you have read have to say on your subject. This will often lead you to develop your own ideas. As you think about which subject and approach to take, look back at the material from classroom lectures, discussions, and assigned readings. If you've been taking good notes in class and on the reading assignments, they're an excellent place to begin.

The organized way to write a paper is better, though it's not always an option. Here you first think systematically about how the essay will eventually be structured, make notes and a tentative outline, and then start to write. Again, keep in mind that even if you already have an outline, *writing is a method of discovery, not a report of what you already know.* The final paper may be quite different from what you expected before sitting down to work out your thinking in detail. I once researched and started to write a book thinking I would end up defending a particular thesis. In the end, after having written and thought about it as I wrote, it became clear that my original idea just would not fly. So I ended up criticizing it and reaching a different conclusion. That is not at all uncommon.

Here is another very helpful suggestion. Good ideas don't just occur when sitting at a desk, so make the whole world your desk. Make notes whenever you are thinking about your subject, whatever you happen to be doing. (I often do this myself.) Norman Davies, author of a massive 1,365-page work entitled *Europe: A History* (Pimlico, 1997), reports in his Preface that his book "has possibly benefited from writing in every sort of inspiring locale—on trains, in planes, in canteens, in hospital waiting-rooms, on Hawaiian beaches, on the back row of other people's seminars, even in a crematorium car park." The lesson is clear: never pass up a chance to jot down whatever ideas, sentences, or even phrases come into your head that you think might be eventually useful. These notes, which may run into paragraphs or even pages, can then be folded into the actual paper when you finally sit down to write. Therefore, it's not a bad idea to have paper and pencil easily available—for instance, next to your bed. You never know when a thought, or even just a well-turned sentence, may occur to you. Don't make the mistake of assuming that you will be able to recall what you're thinking later on; write it down immediately. (I've even been known to get out of the shower to write down some ideas and then get back in.)

If you find the prospect of writing a long paper daunting, it also helps to begin by dividing it into sections and to think of each of those sections as a separate, short essay. Anybody can write a few pages, and a longer essay is nothing more than a bunch of shorter sections strung together. Remember:

you do not need to know how the story will end before you start writing. Writing is about thinking things through, not just putting down what you already think.

NARROWING THE TOPIC: SUBJECT, APPROACH, THESIS

*i*n almost all papers, you need to have a thesis of the appropriate sort, and you need to defend it with reasons. This is true whether your paper is written for history, political science, economics, literature, or philosophy. It's even true for papers in the sciences. As you begin to think through what you want to accomplish in your paper, focus on three questions: What's my subject? What's my approach? What's my thesis?

First, of course, you must ask yourself which *subject* you want to write about. If your instructor assigned a topic, you've got the beginning of an answer. If you don't have an assigned topic, then you will have to choose among the many possibilities: an issue you find interesting, an author or particular essay you've read, or an argument that you'd like to consider in more detail. Once you have a general subject, whether selected by you or by your professor, you need to make it more specific. Merely deciding on a general topic isn't enough. Unless you're more precise, the paper runs the risk of being so broad that it never gets into the issues in any real depth. So whatever subject you choose, it's useful to break it down into a series of subquestions.

After you've identified the subject of the paper, being as precise as you can, next ask yourself which general *approach* to use in discussing your topic. Here again you have many possibilities. You might criticize a particular position or argument, for instance, or develop your own argument on one side or another of the topic. Or you might compare two different positions on the issue, arguing that one is superior to the other. Perhaps you'll want to look at a pair of essays taking different, opposing positions to assess which is stronger. You might decide, for instance, that in the first part of the paper you will just state in your own words another person's position that you think you might want to critique, an argument that you will eventually try to undermine, or two contrasting positions you intend to compare. Then, having explained whatever you intend to discuss in your paper, in the second part you may go on to develop a criticism of it that you think has merit, concluding perhaps with an assessment of that criticism.

Finally, remember that a good paper is usually more than just a summary, however clear and accurate, of other people's thinking on a subject. Before you are done, you'll need to come up with your conclusion, or *thesis*. But you must do more than simply state the thesis: if you haven't already done so, you must also defend it by explaining the reasons why you think your thesis is right. Merely saying "I agree with so-and-so" is not enough; you have to explain *why* you have reached the conclusion you have—that is, you must defend as well as state your thesis.

Remember too that after you have written your paper you will need to be able to complete these three sentences: "The subject of my paper is . . ."; "The approach I take in the paper is . . ."; and "The thesis I defend in the paper is . . ." If you can't do that, and do it briefly and succinctly, then your paper is almost surely not good enough to hand in.

Which brings me to the next topic: how to write a *good* paper. Regardless of the method you used to get started—the "just do it" or the organized method—your goal is to produce an essay on time and in a way that is personally satisfying, intellectually beneficial, *and* worthy of a good grade. There is no magic formula for achieving these objectives, because each student brings her own particular abilities, experience, and personality to the task of writing papers.

WHAT PROFESSORS LOOK FOR IN A PAPER

*b*asically, what professors look for is a *well-organized, clearly structured paper that explains and defends an identifiable thesis with a degree of originality or insight.* More specifically, in my experience most professors weigh these five factors as they read and grade papers (but not necessarily in this order of importance): (1) effort, (2) mastery of the material, (3) sound organizational structure, (4) persuasiveness, and (5) good writing (including language, punctuation, grammar, and spelling). I'll save the last topic, writing quality, for later chapters.

Effort

Has the author worked sufficiently hard researching and writing the essay?

Although it's not always explicitly stated, most people who grade papers appreciate hard work and seriousness of purpose, so that effort often translates into higher grades. You show this effort by producing a well-researched, carefully argued paper, of course, but also by the attention you pay to the little things in your paper, such as spelling, footnotes, and typographical errors.

Mastery of the Material

Does the writer show a good grasp of the lectures, reading assignments, and other material used as background for the paper?

Here it's useful to recall the earlier discussion of how to read and understand what you are reading. It is important in writing to avoid misinterpretations of lectures and readings and to show that you have worked hard to see as deeply into your material as you possibly can.

Sound Organizational Structure

Does the paper proceed in a logical, clear, and coherent fashion?

Is the paper's structure evident to the reader? Sound, clear organization is a trait of every good paper. For many papers, it is not uncommon for professors to conclude that while the content is well researched or insightful, the essay is poorly organized. First I'll say something about structure; then I'll make some suggestions about how to write a well-organized paper.

Your paper will consist of a number of components, perhaps with some components nested inside others. Each component should play its part in the whole. You need to think about the different parts of the paper and how they fit together to make a single, coherent argument on behalf of your thesis. I suggest you start by thinking in terms of three segments:

1. The *introduction,* in which you try to arouse your reader's interest and set out in general terms your answer to the question posed by the paper.

2. The *main body,* in which you analyze the work of others and develop an argument to justify what *you* think.

3. The *conclusion,* in which you briefly restate the argument, giving an overview of where you began, where you ended up, and how you got there.

Keep this basic structure or outline of your argument in mind as you write, being as clear as possible at each step along the way about what you are trying to establish and how you propose to do it. Make that organizational structure as clear as you can.

Don't hide the ball from the reader. Since you want the reader to be able to understand precisely what you want to say, the title and first paragraph bear careful thought. The first sentence of the paper is often the most important, so think hard about what you want it to say. Pay careful attention to the conclusion as well. Taken together, these can create a strong, lasting impression on the reader.

Be sure also, as you reach the end, to provide the reader with a recap of your major points. Summarize your paper, stating its thesis and the major arguments you used to defend it. If you compared different authors, summarize the important similarities and differences you uncovered.

Never be tempted by the familiar thought "I understand what I mean; I just can't say it." Until you can say it or, better still, put it on paper, you don't *really* understand it. That's why writing is often difficult—and important—work.

Finally, after you have finished, you may find that you did not end up where you expected. That's fine; as I have said, writing is a method of discovery, not a report on what you already know. If that happens, be sure to rewrite the introduction so you actually accomplish in the paper what you claim you do at the beginning.

Persuasiveness

Is the paper well reasoned?

Remember as you write that your task is to convince the reader that your thesis is correct by giving good reasons. A good essay does not just go on and on about a topic; it must lead toward a conclusion—that is, it must have various distinguishable stages, and movement between them must be justified on the basis of logic and evidence. For that reason, skills you have developed reading and understanding what you read, identifying the argument structure, and critically evaluating what you have read are just as important here, when you construct your own paper.

The simplest form of argument is one that advances from stage to stage in a linear fashion, but you will often wish to devise more complex arguments. For example, you may need to establish each of the propositions A, B, and C to reach your conclusion, D. Whatever the structure of the argument, essays have to be written in a linear form with one sentence following another, so what you may have to do is establish A, B, and C in turn and then give very clear signs that you are appealing to all three in moving on to establish D. If your paper compares or contrasts two different positions or authors or analyzes critically the view of another writer, you will still be trying to show that your comparison is fruitful and your interpretation correct by giving evidence from the texts. A major factor in the success of an essay is the extent to which the movements between stages of an argument are sound. One key to this success is avoiding errors in reasoning, of which (as we discussed in Chapter 4) there are many varieties.

On the positive side, moving from stage to stage in the argument does not require that your position be unassailable—just clear and well supported. Nobody starts an argument from scratch, so making assumptions is not, in itself, objectionable. However, the assumptions should at least be plausible, and the essay should make them explicit. If they are controversial, you have two options: (1) defend them or (2) simply acknowledge that you know they are controversial but say you will nonetheless assume their truth for purposes of argument in the paper.

Before you are finished, think about the most important *objections to your own view.* How might somebody object to your thesis? Then ask yourself whether you think that objection is serious and should be addressed. How might you best answer the objection? Finally, remember that it's always better to acknowledge an objection (and so get credit for seeing it) even if you cannot respond completely. You should be honest in your paper. Nothing says you cannot admit that there are problems with your argument. If you cannot adequately answer an objection, you might still conclude that the balance of reasons supports your position, despite its admitted weaknesses. Or you might simply acknowledge the existence of an objection or problem, leaving it to another day (or paper) to consider its merits.

Good Writing

I'll set this important topic aside, leaving it to be discussed in subsequent chapters on language, grammar, and punctuation. First, I want to say something about some of the more mechanical aspects of writing, such as how to handle outside sources and quotations and the layout of the paper.

SOURCES AND DOCUMENTATION

*e*ven though this is an area where students are often at their worst, it's among the easiest writing problems to get right. All you have to do is pay attention and be a little careful. The purpose of citations is to give your reader these pieces of information: the author's name or names, the date of publication, the title of the work, and information about where the work was published. You can use various citation forms when you provide references to secondary sources: footnotes, endnotes, and author–date references in the text. Each has its advantages. I think the easiest is the author–date method, though some people prefer to see footnotes at the bottom of each page or endnotes. Your professor may prefer one or the other method.

Author–Date Method

In the *author–date method,* you simply put the author's name and date of publication inside parentheses within the text, after the quotation, and then give the complete citation at the end of the paper under the heading "References" or "Bibliography." Nothing appears at the bottom of the page as with the footnote method.

Citations within the text. Within the body of the text, place references in parentheses. Identify the author, date of publication, and the page numbers, if relevant. A citation will look like this:

(Author date: page numbers).

For example, if you quote Tom Jones in his 1978 book, *My Great Book,* you would simply put the author's name followed by the date and the page number after the quotation:

As Tom Jones claims, "The world is a wonderful place" (Jones 1978: 17).

If you don't quote directly but instead refer to the work more generally, do it this way:

As Jones (1978) argues, the world is a fine place in which to live.

Be sure you refer to the author, not to the editor, of the book from which the material came. If you are quoting from an article in an anthology of different authors, use the author's name and the date that the original article or book by that author was published, not when the edited book was published. Then, in the bibliographical references at the end, refer to the author of the article and show that you got the article from another book. I describe the form for that in the next section.

Bibliography of works cited. The books and articles you use, whether cited or merely read as background, should be listed alphabetically by author in your bibliography, which appears at the end of your paper. The author's name should be followed by publication date, title, where the reference was published, and the name of the publisher.

Books by a single author look like this:

Lastname, A. (date). *Title.* Place: Publisher.

For example, your reference would be:

Rawls, J. (1971). *A Theory of Justice.* Cambridge: Harvard University Press.

Articles and essays typically appear in either a journal or a collection of essays, usually edited by somebody other than the author. Remember to refer to the author of the article or book, not to the editor, in both the text and the bibliography. When you refer to the article in the text using the author–date method, use the same format as you do with books:

(Author date: page numbers)

Then, in the bibliography, you should proceed as follows. If the essay appeared in a collection, use this method:

> Lastname, A. (date). "Article Title," in A. Name and B. Name (Eds.) *Book Title.* Place: Publisher, pages.

Here's an example using the author–date method citing an article by Smith titled "My Great Essay" in a book edited by Jones:

> Smith, J. (1886). "My Great Essay," in T. Jones (Ed.) *Great Essays of the Western World.* New York: Harper Press, 138–144.

If your article was published in a periodical or journal, use this method:

> Lastname, A. (date). "Article Title," *Journal Name.* vol. #, pages.

Here is an example:

> Sokol, A. (1996). "Transgressing the Boundaries: Toward a Transformative Hermeneutics of Quantum Gravity," *Social Text.* Spring/Summer, 217–252.

If you use this author–date method, you can still use a footnote or endnote for purposes other than citing others' work—for example, to elaborate on or qualify a point you make in the paper.

Edited books are done this way:

> Lastname, A. (Ed.) (Date). *Title.* Place: Publisher.

So you would list a book of Marx's writings edited by David McClellan this way:

> McClellan, D. (Ed.) (1977). *Selected Writings of Karl Marx.* Oxford: Oxford University Press.

But remember that if you referred in your essay to a specific author in a collection, you should use as your reference that author's name, not the editor of the book.

If you have *multiple works by the same author* that you wish to list in your bibliography, use the same style except instead of repeating the name just use a line, like this:

> Jones, T. (1978). *My Great Book.* Cambridge: Harvard University Press.
>
> _____ (1983). *My Second Great Book.* Denver: Cowboy Press.

Footnote and Endnote Methods

Two alternatives to the author-date system are endnotes and footnotes, which are easy to compose in most word processing programs. Here, instead of putting the author and date in the text, you use numbers in the text and then indicate the page and work cited using the same number, either at the bottom of the page (if it's a footnote) or at the end of the paper (if it's an endnote).

To cite a *book written by a single author,* use this format:

1. Firstname Lastname, *Title of Book* (Location: Publisher, date), p. or pp.

For instance, you might say in a footnote or endnote:

1. Tom Hanks, *How to Act* (London: University Press, 2002), p. 871.

Articles in anthologies follow a slightly different format:

2. Firstname Lastname, "Article Title," in *Title of Anthology,* Edition no., Ed. Name (Location: Publisher, date), pages.

So an essay written by Singer in a book edited by me should look like this:

2. Peter Singer, "Rich and Poor," in *Morality and Moral Controversies,* 5th Edition, Ed. John Arthur (Upper Saddle River, NJ: Prentice Hall, 1997), pp. 259–265.

Articles in periodicals follow a similar format:

3. Firstname Lastname, "Title of Article," *Periodicalname,* volume #, periodical # (date of the volume), pages.

Here is an example:

3. James Thomson, "The Meaning of Life," *Journal of Great Thoughts,* 14, 2 (2002), pp. 45–59.

After you have given a full citation in one of the footnotes or endnotes, you can *abbreviate subsequent citations* of the same work this way:

4. Theresa Smith, "The Story of My Life," *Journal of Great Stories,* Vol. 1 (New York: New York University Press, 1988), p. 140.

5. Smith, "Story," p. 141.

Bibliography with footnotes or endnotes. If you need to cite sources you used but did not refer to in a footnote or endnote, then you should use a bibliography. Follow a similar format as you did for the footnotes and endnotes, except begin with the authors' or editors' *last* names, listing them alphabetically. For example:

> Strunk, William J., and E. B. White, *Elements of Style,* 4th Ed. (Boston: Allyn and Bacon, 1999).

Whatever method you use—author–date, footnote, or endnote—here are some important points to keep in mind about using citations.

1. It's often helpful to provide a bibliography at the end, though it is not necessary if you use footnotes or endnotes rather than the author–date method. If you used footnotes or endnotes, you may be required to provide a bibliography if you relied on sources that were not otherwise noted.

2. If you cite an article in an edited book, be sure to cite to the author you are quoting, *not the editor* of the book in which the article appeared.

3. Be consistent in style and punctuation, whatever citation method you choose.

As you have probably gathered, there isn't universal agreement about these issues. Different books on the subject offer different advice about citations and bibliographies (see the list in Appendix I: Additional Resources). So unless your professor says otherwise, my advice is to use your own judgment and choose the system you think works easiest and best for you. Remember that the point of references is to give the reader the relevant information about your sources in a consistent, efficient way that does not detract from the writing quality or flow of the paper.

Citing Electronic Publications and the Internet

Whether you use the author–date method, footnotes, or endnotes, if you use Internet sources it is *critical* that you cite them along with your other sources. (If you are in doubt about the rules, look at the principles of academic honesty discussed in Chapter 8, or at your own university's rules.

Because widespread use of the Internet is so new, no universal agreement exists on the specific form citations should take. Electronic publications are also much easier to change than printed works, so the location names are sometimes different from where you originally found the information. I suggest that you first include all the information that would normally be found in a printed citation (author, title, publication, and date of publication) and then add the date you accessed the site and the Internet address—that is, the universal resource locator (URL) where you found it. Put the Web address in angle brackets: < > That way, the reader will be able to tell not only the author and other information but also where the citation came from and will be able to visit the site. For instance, you would cite an article from an electronic journal this way, beginning with the same format as for a normal journal citation followed by the Web address:

> Firstname Lastname, "Title of Article," *Name of Periodical,* vol. #, periodical # (date). Location of source (if available). Date of access, <Webaddress>.

For example, you would cite an article by Joan Smith titled "On the Uses of the Internet" from the online journal *Internet Studies,* volume 2, number 1, which you looked at most recently on December 15, 2002, this way:

> Joan Smith, "On the Uses of the Internet," *Internet Studies,* 2, 1 (2001). December 15, 2002, <http://www.uta.edu/Internet Studies2_1/ sobstyl.html>.

A citation to an online edition of a newspaper should be cited this way, again following the same basic rules:

> "Affirmative Action Case Goes to Court," *New York Times* on the Web, May 13, 1975. September 22, 2002, <www.NYTimes.com/oped/ links.cohen14,3>.

Statistical or other information found in a database should give the title of the database and the name of the creator (if available), followed by the publication information (institution, date, and so on) and then the date of access and the URL.

If you find an article or chapter on a database, use this format:

> Firstname Lastname, "Title," *Name of Periodical* (date). Name of Database, Location of Database. Date accessed, <URL>.

For instance, an article by Midler would look like this:

> Robert Midler, "Hawthorne's Winter Dreams," *Nineteenth-Century Literature* (Vol. 3, No. 2, 1999). OneFile Binghamton University Library, Binghamton, NY. July 26, 2002, <http://web3.infotrac.galegroup.com>.

Here is an online book, which is a U.S. government publication:

> Elizabeth Peterson, *Changing Faces of Tradition* (Oct. 1996). United States Government, National Endowment for the Arts. August 18, 2002, <http://arts.endow.gov/pub/Researcharts/Folk.html>.

Remember, for more complete information about citations, references, and bibliographies, take a look at one of the books on the subject listed in Appendix I: Additional Resources.

LAYOUT AND PRESENTATION

before turning in a paper ask yourself two final questions: *Does the paper look good? Is it neat and easy to read?* Here are some general suggestions about the layout and presentation of your paper. Some are largely aesthetic, while others will affect not only how the paper looks but sometimes whether or not it is understood. All may influence your final grade, so it's worth a few minutes to ensure the paper looks good.

1. Papers should always be typed, with the pages stapled at the top left-hand corner.

2. Number the pages consecutively.

3. The front page, or *cover sheet,* should include your name, the essay title, the course name, the date, and the name of your professor.

4. Leave margins of at least one inch at the top, bottom, and sides. The grader needs this space for comments and questions.

5. Use double spacing between lines and a normal typesize (12 is most common) that results in around 300 words per page.

Most word processing programs have spell-check capacities, which you should use to check through your essay. You need never make another spelling error again! In using the spell-check, however, remember that you need to consult a dictionary when you have the slightest doubt as to the meaning of a word. You may quite easily think you understand a word from the context in which you have read it, but the word actually may mean something quite different. Also remember that you might be consistently using a wrong spelling for an intended word that happens to be the correct spelling of an unintended word, so the spell-check cannot detect it. For example, you might type "sight" when you should have typed "cite." No spell-check can check for meaning, so no substitute exists for carefully reading through your essay to pick out missing words, words in the wrong order, and so on. On a more positive note, you can use the spell-check to improve your spelling by noting where you have made a mistake. Take your time when using the spell-check and consciously try to remember the corrections.

Many word processors also contain a thesaurus, which enables you to find words with a similar or related meaning to a given word. Most also give antonyms. This is handy for improving your writing style since it allows you to avoid using the same word too often and can spur your thinking. But it can also mislead if you simply substitute an unfamiliar word without checking a dictionary. (For example, one word processor's thesaurus gives "élan" as a synonym for "style," but making that substitution in the third sentence of this paragraph would be a mistake.)

Neat layout and presentation is no alternative to good content and structure, of course, but it can help readers follow the structure of your essay. For example, if you have developed a thesis and defended it in a way that seems to you robust and logical, make sure that the reader sees that by distinguishing headings, subheadings, and sub-subheadings. Similarly, use of boldface, italics, or underlining in the text can emphasize crucial points. But be sure to be consistent when you use these—and don't go overboard.

Be sure you keep your computer disks and directories well organized and safely stored. One way of doing this is to have a directory or a floppy disk for each course or one for each semester with a directory that distinguishes each course. Also be sure to back up your work. If you are using shared computers provided by the university, you should save files onto a working disk and then back it all up on second disk. Always make backups; it is discouraging to lose work when a disk goes bad—and if you write enough, it will eventually happen, if it hasn't already! Put your name and address on each disk in case you lose it.

THE REAL SECRET TO GOOD WRITING: EDITING AND REVISING

*J*onathan Bennett, a well-known philosopher and an excellent writer, once described to a graduate student the advice he had been given by another famous writer:

Gilbert Ryle once told me, "What doesn't read well to the ear doesn't read well to the eye," and that changed my life. More than any other one thing, that insight showed me how to start climbing out of the garbage pit up into the plain of decent prose. I had some of my material read to me while I listened with my eyes closed, was appalled by how ugly and boring it was, and took action. I no longer use exactly this technique, but I read aloud to myself everything I write for publication. I recently sat in my study at home and read my book *The Act Itself* aloud in ringing tones, imagining an audience and aiming to do the performance with gusto. Whenever my confidence ebbed and my voice wavered because the prose was not moving properly, I re-wrote. For your first few professional years, though, I urge you to submit yourself to the discipline of listening to your own prose without at the same time following it on the page. It may well be the worst experience of your intellectual life. If so, it will also be one of the most valuable.[1]

First and foremost, remember this rule: *The best way, if not the only way, to learn how to write well is to learn how to edit well.* No paper, regardless of how often it has been revised, is ever so well written or its thesis so well established that it would not benefit from further editing and rewriting. People who publish books and papers revise them over and over before they are finally published. So it should be obvious that students, too, should *never* pass in a paper that has not been *rewritten completely at least once.* Doing this requires that your paper be done early. Nobody who writes all night and hands in a just completed paper will have written anything close to his or her best. Ideally, you should leave yourself at least a day to let the paper sit before you pick it up to edit it and make revisions. Sometimes the revisions will be substantial, so leave yourself enough time.

Learning to edit is not simple, but it is also not terribly hard—and is certainly not impossible. The secret is to learn to look at your own work as if you did not write it and to go over it word by word, line by line. As you do, ask yourself if what you have just said makes sense or if it would make sense to somebody reading it for the first time. Then look for wordiness and lack of precision by asking yourself: Is this word necessary? Does it say just what I want? Does it even make sense? Is there a better way to express the idea? How might it be expressed more clearly? (All of these subjects are discussed in the following chapters dealing with language use, grammar, and punctuation.)

Often, as I sit down with a student who has not done well on a paper and I start reading the paper aloud to the student, it becomes perfectly clear to *both* of us that whatever the student was thinking at the time did not get expressed clearly on paper. Reading aloud is an excellent test to help decide how well written your paper is.

Keep in mind, too, that one of the most important skills you should try to develop as a writer is to be able to explain what you want to say in a different way. Such restatements are often invaluable to readers struggling to follow what you are saying in a paper. Sometimes you may decide the second statement is better and the first unnecessary. Other times you may decide you want to keep both versions as an additional aid to the reader. Be sure, however, to watch for bloated language and redundancy. It is almost always better to shorten a paper. (Again, I have much more to say about this in later chapters.)

---

[1]Jonathan Bennet and Samuel Gorovitz, "Improving Academic Writing," *Teaching Philosophy,* vol. 20, no. 2 (June 1997), p. 128.

Besides reviewing the writing, you should also confirm that the paper is well organized by outlining it. You can use the same approach you did when outlining assigned readings. An outline is an excellent diagnostic tool, since it forces you to focus on the paper's overall organization. You may be surprised (pleasantly or not) at what you learn when you do it.

Along with asking how your writing and organization can be improved, you should also think about whether the arguments in the paper are good ones. Your outline will be helpful, since it should uncover the paper's basic argumentative structure. As you read and outline the paper in preparation for your final revision, keep in mind what I said earlier about understanding what you are reading (see Chapter 5).

Finally, never turn in a paper with silly errors of grammar, spelling, punctuation, or word choice. There is no excuse for this, and it often results in a lowered grade. Your paper represents your mind: you don't want it, *or you,* to seem superficial, sloppy, confused, or dull. So if you have doubts about grammar, punctuation, spelling, or the meaning of a word, check the relevant parts of this book or refer to another appropriate resource listed in Appendix I: Additional Resources.

Review Questions and Exercises

1. What are the different ways to get started writing a paper?
2. Why is editing the real key to being a good writer?

The Rules of the Road

cheating and academic honesty

WHY HONESTY MATTERS

Professors take academic honesty seriously. I know this from my own experiences as a professor and as a member of academic honesty committees. Universities depend on adherence to principles of intellectual honesty and integrity by faculty, staff, and students. Actions that breach these principles erode the trust of those who look to universities for honest evaluations of academic work arrived at through honest processes. Violations that breach these principles may cause individual harm, including incorrect evaluations of performance and inaccurate reports to postgraduate schools, professional societies, and employers.

Some universities and colleges have honor codes that require students to report violations. If students learn about but don't report a violation, they have violated the code themselves. Other times, enforcement is left to faculty and administrators.

However it is enforced, your college or university will probably have a code. Penalties for violating that are often severe, resulting in failing the class, suspension, or expulsion. So I encourage you to get a copy of your own code. Sometimes, however, a particular code is not very specific, and students can be left confused about what is required. That can lead to serious trouble.

In general, academic dishonesty involves misappropriation of academic or intellectual credit to oneself or to the discredit of others. A major concern of faculty is whether students violate rules governing plagiarism. Papers often rely on secondary sources—other works on the subject that are quoted directly or used as general references. There's nothing wrong with using outside sources, though different professors have different expectations on the subject. If in doubt, check with your instructor. Some don't encourage or even allow outside sources; other may expect you to use them.

Both copyright law and academic ethics demand that whenever you use someone else's work, you acknowledge that source in your paper. This is especially true when you quote directly. But even if you do not use the exact language, it's still plagiarism if you represent somebody else's ideas as your own. Think of it as a kind of fraud perpetrated against your professor, fellow students, and the overall academic community. Professors who discover plagiarism often fail the student; other times students are sent before ethics boards and sometimes expelled or suspended from the university. As I said, we take plagiarism seriously.

Plagiarism is sometimes committed by mistake (I had it happen just this past semester). It occurs when a student copies word for word from a book without using quotation marks. If you quote directly, it is not enough to footnote the sentence: *anytime you copy words, you must use quotation marks to indicate that the words are not your own.* I have included in the next section a sample code explaining the various forms of plagiarism. You should familiarize yourself with it.

PRINCIPLES OF ACADEMIC HONESTY

*m*ost universities have policies that define academic honesty, and professors watch carefully to see that students do not violate these important academic standards. If you haven't done so already, you should familiarize yourself with your own university's policies. They are usually readily available; if not, ask your professor to see them. I have included in this section a list of the principles of academic honesty I use in my classes; this is a code that I and other committee members wrote for Binghamton University last year. Our goal was to describe what we believe to be widely accepted standards of academic honesty. The code explains in detail what most universities and professors regard as the basic rules governing student conduct as well as the rules governing professors and students engaged in research. Keep in mind, however, that no set of written guidelines can anticipate all types and degrees of violations of academic honesty; thus the following is only a summary. Your university or college may have its own additional requirements; for example, it may have an honor code requiring you to turn other students in if you find them violating the principles. This list does, however, give a good overview of the basic rules governing academic honesty.

Plagiarism

Plagiarism is presenting the work of another person as one's own work (including papers, words, ideas, information, computer code, data, evidence, organizing principles, or style of presentation of someone else taken from the Internet, books, periodicals, or other sources). Plagiarism includes quoting, paraphrasing, or summarizing (even a few phrases) without acknowledgment; failing to acknowledge the source of either a major idea or an ordering principle central to one's own paper; relying on another person's data, evidence, or critical method; submitting another student's work as one's own; and using unacknowledged research sources gathered by someone else.

Cheating on Examinations

Cheating on examinations involves giving or receiving unauthorized help before, during, or after an examination. Examples of unauthorized help include collaborating of any sort during an examination; reading an exam before it has been given; using notes, books, tapes, computers, or other aids during an examination; allowing another person to take an examination in one's place; looking at someone else's examination during the examination period; allowing another person to use one's own examination during the examination period; and passing examination information to students who have not yet taken the exam.

Multiple Submissions

Multiple submissions involves submitting substantial portions of the same work for credit more than once, unless the student has the prior explicit consent of the instructor(s) to whom the material is being or has been submitted.

Forgery

Forgery is imitating another person's signature on academic documents (for example, an academic advising form or one's own paper that is signed with respect to the time of submission) or other official documents that affect academic credit (for example, a medical form submitted in support of taking a makeup exam).

Sabotage

Sabotage is deliberately impairing, destroying, damaging, or stealing another's work or working material. Examples include destroying, stealing, or damaging another's lab experiment, computer program, term paper, exam, or project; removing uncharged library material so that others cannot use them; defacing or damaging library material so that others cannot use them; and hoarding or displacing materials within the library so that others have undue difficulty using them.

Unauthorized Collaboration

Unauthorized collaboration is collaboration on papers or other academic assignments that has not been explicitly authorized by the instructor.

Fabrication and Misrepresentation

This involves the misrepresentation or fabrication of sources, the justification of absences, late assignments, and other activities.

Bribery

Bribery is offering any service or article of value to an instructor or teaching assistant with the purpose or effect of receiving a grade or other academic benefit that was not earned on the merits of the academic work.

language use

MEMORABLE EXAMPLES OF BAD (AND GOOD) WRITING

Before turning to our topic—good writing and its importance—here are some fun and interesting examples of bad writing. They are all real.

Instructions for assembling an IKEA desk: "It is advisory to be two people during assembly."

A sign on a street: *"I Lost 40 lbs. in Two Months. Call for Free Samples!"*

Another sign in a grocery store in my own town of Binghamton, New York: *"Not all of our apples are sprayed with alar."*

Story from the *Akron Beacon Journal*: *"Police find man dead to death in a motel."*

An exchange between a lawyer and a witness who was being cross-examined:

Lawyer: "Is it not true that on June 15 you were not at your office?"

Witness: "Yes."

Lawyer: "Yes, what?"

Witness: "Yes, it is not true."

Lawyer: "What is not true?"

On the other extreme, here's a wonderful example of how writing can be improved and turned into great writing. It involves Abraham Lincoln's efforts to craft his First Inaugural Address. Secretary of State William Henry Seward thought Lincoln's draft of the speech needed to be less strident, so Seward suggested to Lincoln that he add the following concluding paragraph, written by Seward:

> I close. We are not, we must not be, aliens or enemies but fellow country-men and brethren. . . . The mystic chords which proceeding from so many battlefields and so many patriot graves pass through all the hearts and all the hearths in this broad continent of ours will yet again harmonize in their ancient music when breathed upon by the guardian angel of the nation.

After reading this, Lincoln rewrote it into these memorable lines.

> I am loath to close. We are not enemies, but friends. We must not be ene-mies. . . . The mystic chords of memory, stretching from every battlefield, and patriot grave, to every living heart and hearthstone, all over this broad land, will yet swell the chorus of the Union, when again touched, as surely they will be, by the better angels of our nature.[1]

As you think about how to improve your own writing, take a minute to study these two passages carefully, noting the specific changes Lincoln made to Seward's draft. This example illustrates nicely the power and importance of writing well and how rewriting can improve a first draft. It also shows how much it can help to have a classmate or friend critique your paper before you're done—even if that person is not a better writer than you are. Without Seward's bumbling suggestions, Lincoln would almost surely not have added that magnificent closing to his speech.

In this and the chapters that follow, you will find many suggestions for improving your writing, including language use, punctuation, and grammar. I've also listed some commonly misspelled words that keep showing up in my students' papers. In practice, avoiding most of the common errors is not

---

[1]Both examples are from Gary Wills, *Lincoln at Gettysburg* (New York: Simon and Schuster, 1992), p. 158.

difficult. It's mostly a matter of paying attention. Remember: if you don't, your professors will.

ADEQUATE IS GOOD[2]

*O*ne of the great writers of the English language, Samuel Johnson, once observed: "What is written without effort is in general read without pleasure" (*Johnsonian Miscellanies,* Two Birkbeck Hill, 1897). I believe that is absolutely true. Very few people write truly well, and among those who do, even fewer do it without sustained effort.

Perhaps the most serious error students and others make in writing is to think that they have to be good or even great writers, often knowing all the while that they are really only adequate. That attitude makes people miserable and sometimes causes problems even getting started (what is sometimes called "writers' block"). It also can lead to bad writing, because students don't do what they can do, which is to write an adequate paper in clear, simple sentences. By trying to do too much and be too fancy, they actually make it worse. I encourage you to start with the idea that you are going to do what you can do, which is write adequately, and are not going to hand in a paper that is less than adequately written in all respects. That is a difficult enough task for almost everybody. Do not try to make your writing great by using big words, for example, or fancy punctuation, unless you are certain what you have produced is adequately written. Even then I would advise sticking with clearly and simply phrased sentences using language you are comfortable with in everyday conversation (and therefore understand). If you feel discouraged about your writing, it's useful to recall Johnson's comment.

WHY RULES MATTER

*S*ometimes people who are skeptical about rules of language, grammar, spelling, and punctuation like to point out that such rules are not "written in heaven," nor are they even laws of nature. Indeed, these people say, they change. What was once thought incorrect and unacceptable may become required, or vice versa. I agree with that, of course. Language and other rules do change over time, and they are not laws of nature. But what does not follow from that point, as people sometimes think, is that rules don't matter or that we should pay no attention to them. Rules governing language, grammar, and spelling are like the rules of chess or baseball. Without the rules, there would be no game at all. So while it is also

---

[2]I owe this point, that adequate is good, to discussions with my wife, Amy.

true that baseball rules evolve and change, to say that we can ignore them is tantamount to saying we can get along without the game of baseball. But getting along without baseball is far easier to imagine than human beings getting along without language, since human life, at least as we know it, would not exist without language. We need it to have what we call civilization, including everything from culture to morality and law.

So playing by the rules of the game is not just a nice thing to do. If I weren't following all the complex rules governing the meaning and use of words, grammar, and punctuation, you would have no idea what I was saying—because I would not, in fact, be saying anything. If you sometimes wonder if rules about language usage, spelling, punctuation, and grammar matter, ask yourself whether such rules as driving on the right (or left), using turn signals, and obeying stop signs and solid yellow lines in the road are really important. In my opinion, the rules of language matter much more than traffic rules (though both are important!).

Good writing also is important in many other ways. Few problems are more annoying to professors or other readers (or more complained about by employers) than errors in language usage or mistakes in grammar, punctuation, and spelling. Some of the mistakes discussed here and in the following chapters are merely irritating, but others can make text that seems perfectly clear to you, the writer, into absolute gobbledygook to the reader. No one wants to have to reread a passage several times to find out what a writer is trying to say. However painstaking the research or thoughtful the argument, a badly expressed essay is a bad essay: it fails to convey its author's thoughts to the reader.

Writing is a craft, and like any craft, it improves with practice. The most important first step in improving your writing is to become aware of how you practice the craft; learn to notice, and study, your own writing style. Pay attention to your use of words and whether you repeat certain ones too often. Notice how long your sentences are, and try to vary them. Reading good writers and trying to figure out what makes them good can also be a big help. Having gotten a better sense of your own strengths and weaknesses, you'll be in position to make improvements.

VERBOSITY AND WORDINESS

*U*sing too many words to say what needs saying is a common problem, and not just in students' papers. The basic rule to follow is this: *If it's possible to cut a word, do it; if you can eliminate many words, even better.* Students are sometimes verbose because they're afraid they won't be able to write a long enough paper. That is an error. If you can fulfill the requirements of the assignment in a short, succinct paper, by all means do it (think of Lincoln). If you haven't done enough research or put enough thought into the topic, just throwing in more words won't help. It will make things worse.

Here are some examples, many from essays I've received from students. In each case, the second example is shorter—and better.

> Dworkin brings forth quite relevant questions.
> **Better:** Dworkin raises relevant questions.

> The aim of this essay is to give an understanding of Thomson's view of abortion.
> **Better:** This essay analyzes Thomson's view of abortion.

> They are all of the opinion that it was wrong.
> **Better:** They agree it was wrong.

> Locke wrote two centuries prior to the time Nozick wrote.
> **Better:** Locke wrote two centuries before Nozick.

> Hart should recognize the distinction between rules and principles.
> **Better:** Hart should distinguish between rules and principles.
> **Better still:** Hart should distinguish rules from principles.

> Singer provided a response to Locke's position.
> **Better:** Singer responded to Locke.

> This is a solution that raises many problems.
> **Better:** This solution raises many problems.

> I could not believe the fact that . . .
> **Better:** I could not believe that . . .

> The reason why I disagree with this conclusion is . . .
> **Better:** I disagree with this conclusion because . . .
> **Better still:** I reject this conclusion because . . .

> There is no doubt that . . .
> **Better:** Undoubtedly . . .
> **Better still:** Leave it out altogether. If the point is that obvious, the reader will know it without being told.

The answer lies in the respect that . . .

Better: The answer is that . . .

I can't help but believe . . .

Better: I must believe . . .

Another way to reduce wordiness is to avoid redundant words and phrases, including "I believe that . . . ," "In fact it is the case that . . . ," and "It's important to note that . . ." These may occasionally be useful, but more often they add nothing but words.

BLOATED, IMPRECISE LANGUAGE

Some students think that better writing means writing with longer, more unusual, and more sophisticated sounding words. It doesn't, at least not usually. That is especially true when there is a simpler, more precise way of expressing what is otherwise bloated, vague, and unclear. One of my favorite examples of bloated language is from George Orwell, who targeted bureaucrats and other speakers of "modern" English. In his article "Politics and the English Language," he takes a passage from *Ecclesiastes* and rewrites it in "modern" English.

Original: I returned and saw under the sun, that the race is not to the swift, nor the battle to the strong, neither yet bread to the wise, nor riches to men of understanding, nor yet favor to men of skill; but time and chance happeneth to them all.

Orwell's "Modern" English translation: Objective considerations of contemporary phenomena compels the conclusion that success or failure in competitive activities exhibits no tendency to be commensurate with innate capacity, but that a considerable element of the unpredictable must invariably be taken into account.

This translation may sound smarter—until you think about it. Don't make the common mistake of thinking that you will improve your writing by using a longer or more sophisticated word ("elevating my language," as one of my students once described it). Often the word you look up, though listed as a synonym, will not be used correctly in your paper. The best way to learn to use language is to read, so if you aren't familiar with a word, use one you do understand. Finally, ask yourself if you would ever talk in the way you are writing. If not, then that may indicate that you aren't writing well, or even adequately.

Here are some examples of bloated, pretentious prose rewritten into clear English. Many have turned up in my own students' papers. (Notice their similarity with Orwell's "modern English" translation of *Ecclesiastes*.)

Objective considerations compel the conclusion that . . .

Better: It is reasonable to conclude that . . .

Better still: In conclusion . . . (or Thus . . .)

Although liberalism purports to effect a neutral reconciliation between . . .

Better: Although liberalism claims to reconcile . . .

He declared a realization that the problem was solved.

Better: He said the problem was solved.

Mill's utilization of the harm principle . . .

Better: Mill's use of the harm principle . . .

Don't think undergraduates have a monopoly on bloated, obscure language. The following appeared on a student flier promoting some graduate students' candidacies for the Graduate Student Organization Executive Board. To appreciate the verbosity, try explaining what it means in your own words.

> Our aim is to implode centralized power and disseminate it to more localized sites. We may have to negotiate the parameters between acquiring "teaching experience" and becoming a free or underpaid laborer.

Finally, not to ignore my own field, here are a few sentences from a professional journal. Though most philosophers reject this sort of nonsense, unfortunately some do not. Again, see if you can translate the following passage into clear, concise English.

> The temptation that resides within—as well as presides over—the strategy of an introduction envisages the type of coverage that provides a history. The temptation therefore harbors and seeks to enact the restrictive and restricting borders of an historical continuity. (Though it is one where both history and the nature of continuity remain, of necessity, unexamined.)[3]

---

[3]From Jean-Francois Lyotard, "In Lieu of an Introduction," in *The Lyotard Reader*, Andrew Benjamin, Ed. (Oxford: Blackwell Publishing, 1989), p. xv.

Whatever the merits of the ideas being expressed, the writing is far from clear, succinct, and easy to interpret. Anybody trying to follow this would be obliged to struggle to discover the author's meaning, a challenge not not characteristic of good writing.

The fact that academic writing is sometimes worse than bad, bordering on nonsense, was confirmed when a physicist named Alan Sokal wrote his own made-up parody of such writing and sent it to a journal. In reality, the article was complete gibberish, though it used terms and made claims that are familiar to scholars who term themselves "post-modern." Not knowing the author wrote it as a parody of bad writing, and that it made no sense, the journal published it. Sokal then announced the hoax, much to the embarrassment of the editors.[4]

CONFUSION ABOUT MEANING

*t*he rule here is simple: *Be sure you use words correctly and that they mean precisely what you want them to mean.* As a general proposition, this is uncontroversial; who could disagree? But in fact, it is both difficult and important to use words properly. Students often misuse words in their papers. In this section I describe some of the most common mistakes. Remember: if you're in doubt about a word's meaning, look it up in a dictionary or thesaurus.

Perhaps the most troubling error students make is to use a word whose meaning does not fit with the subject. Here's an example from a paper I recently received:

> **Incorrect:** It raises some points that are imperative for a system to function fairly.

> **Correct:** It raises some problems that must be solved for a system to function fairly.

The test to use here is simple: focus your attention on the words, and ask whether what you are saying makes sense. Do they belong together? In this example, the student in effect said of a "point" that it is "imperative." That makes little sense. Taking some action may be "imperative" or not, and a

---

[4]For a detailed account of the experience and the lessons Sokal takes from it, see Alan Sokal and Jean Bricmont, *Fashionable Nonsense: Postmodern Philosophers' Abuse of Science* (Picador, 1998). Among those lessons is that far too much writing, especially in the humanities and social sciences, is obscure to the point of incomprehensibility, and that much of academe is woefully ignorant of science.

"point" may be important to recognize. But a point can't be imperative. Don't confuse the meanings.

Here's an instance of the failure of subject and verb to fit together semantically:

Incorrect: The benefits of the theory ground its general acceptance.

But ask yourself: does it make sense to say of a "benefit" that it "grounds" something? A premise can "ground" a conclusion, or the existence of a benefit might "warrant" or "justify" an action. So what the student should have written is something closer to this:

Correct: The benefits of the theory justify accepting it.

Also correct: Scientists use the benefits of the theory to justify their acceptance of it.

The best way to avoid this common mistake is to think carefully about the precise meaning of the words you've chosen. Often, as in these cases, the subject or verb used is not the right one, leading to ambiguity and confusion.

Watch Out for Success Concepts

Another problem students encounter involves what are often called "success concepts." For example, to say the writer "refuted" an argument means that the argument was clearly shown to be mistaken. Unless you go on in your paper to show that, it is better to say the writer "argued against the position" or "tried to refute it" or even "disputed" it. Another success concept is "prove." If you claim to have proven something, you are saying more than that you *tried* to prove it; *you claim to have succeeded.*

Be Careful Ascribing Human Feelings or Beliefs to Inanimate Objects

This is especially tempting when the object is your own paper. It's usually better to refer to the person who made the object. Here are two examples:

Incorrect: The book hoped that war could be avoided.
Correct: The author hoped that war could be avoided.

Incorrect: The essay claimed that the argument was mistaken.
Correct: Jones claimed that the argument was mistaken.

Do Not Say "Being That"
When You Mean "Since" or "Is"

One recent student wrote this phrase in a paper:

> The first example being that . . .

He should have said:

> The first example is . . .

Avoid Overusing such Words
as "Very" and "Extremely"

Often a sentence is stronger without the word. This is especially true for strong words, such as "brilliant" or "exceptional." At best, "very" is wasted; at worst, it weakens what you want to say.

Keep in Mind That Some Words Can't
Be Modified by Words like "Very"

"Unique," for instance, means the only one of its kind. Things cannot be *very* unique. It was reported recently in a letter to the editor of the *New York Times* that Microsoft Word's grammar check allowed the writer get away with "a most unique woman," which made the editor quite unhappy. How, he asked, is it possible for anybody to be "most" unique? Other times, adding modifiers is redundant or worse: *very* gorgeous, *extremely* authoritarian, and *extraordinary* genius, for instance.

Don't Confuse "Which" and "That"

The especially careful wordsmith will want to keep this in mind: "that" is a restrictive pronoun and "which" is not restrictive, so you should keep these two usages distinct. Here is an illustration:

> The television that is black and white is in the attic.
>
> The television, which is black and white, is in the attic.

The second sentence says something about the one television; the first sentence, using "that," implies there are other televisions.

CHOOSING YOUR PRONOUN AND VERB TENSE

O ne question you should settle on is how you intend to address the reader. Will you speak directly, as I am doing here, or will the essay be in the third person? Academic writers commonly speak directly, in the second person, to their audiences; if you find that comfortable, I think you should do it. If you don't, be sure to avoid introducing awkward expressions to avoid the first person. For instance, say "As discussed earlier" rather than "As the reader will recall," or "Evolution provides an answer" rather than "In the opinion of this writer, evolution provides an answer."

To identify yourself in the paper, you use the first person. There's nothing wrong with saying "I will argue that . . ." or "I disagree with that conclusion." This is much better than forcing yourself into such statements as "This paper will argue . . ." or "The conclusion will be that X is mistaken." Avoiding first person is often weaker and can lead to using the dreaded passive voice. But again, if you want to avoid first person and keep yourself in the background, at least be consistent. Don't speak sometimes of "the paper" claiming and other times of you claiming.

Using inconsistent verb tenses is another common mistake in papers. When discussing another's work, it's best to use present tense, no matter how long ago the work appeared. So instead of talking about what Mill "wrote," speak of what he "writes" or "says." Most importantly, whatever you choose, stick to it. Don't bounce around mixing these words up:

"argued" and "argues"

"said" and "says"

"wrote" or "has written" and "writes"

If your usual style is to use present tense, you are then free to use the past when appropriate. For example, you may want to make a specific point about an earlier work while discussing a later one: "Mill argued in an early essay that X, though he asserts in *On Liberty* that Y."

"SEXIST" LANGUAGE AND THE GENDERED PRONOUN

i n most books these days, it's called "sexist" for people to follow the historic English use of "he" to mean "he or she," "mankind" to mean "humanity," and "him" to refer to "him or her." I am dubious about this charge, however. Not that there isn't such a thing as sexist language: using statements like "This is a woman's argument" to mean the argument is weak is obviously unacceptable. A few words and expressions do imply male superiority. For instance, don't use "emasculate" as a synonym for "weaken" (try "eviscerate" instead). Similarly, "manly" is not a good synonym for "courageous." In general, though, the problem is that, unlike many languages, English has no neuter personal pronouns. There is no way to avoid gender identification if you want the convenience of using a pronoun instead of repeating the proper noun. For instance, instead of saying "The President sent the President's bill to Congress," you must say either "his bill" or "her bill" as appropriate. While in cases like this, the problem is not acute since the specific gender is known, what do you do when you don't know?

Standard usage for centuries has been to assume that a person of unknown gender is male. However, many thoughtful people now avoid this construction because the people referred to are often not males. I think that the best solution is simply to avoid constructions where "he" refers to a single person of indeterminate sex. If you are a good writer, you can almost always find a way to do this without damaging your writing style. If it can't be done, it's now fairly standard to alternate use of "he" and "she" in discussions and examples. Or, you may resort to the sometimes clunky "he or she" or "his or her." "Each student turned in his or her paper" is becoming more acceptable but should still be avoided, if possible. For example, you might change the sentence to "All the students have turned in their papers." Or here's another example:

> **Incorrect:** Has everybody on the team gotten their ice cream?
>
> **A less than ideal solution:** Has everybody on the team gotten his or her ice cream?

It's best to rewrite the sentence as follows:

> **Correct:** Have all the team members gotten their ice cream?

Here are some other examples of good, neutral alternatives.

ORIGINAL WORD OR PHRASE	A BETTER ALTERNATIVE
mankind	humanity, men and women
chairman	chairwoman or chairman; chairperson or chair, if unknown
man	person
the man in the street	people in general
man-made	synthetic, manufactured
to a man	everyone, unanimously
policeman	police officer; policewoman or policeman, if gender is known
fireman	firefighter
founding fathers	founders

The whole issue of gender in writing can be put in perspective by keeping in mind your purposes: you are writing to communicate, and you are reading to understand. Thus, if you are writing for readers you think may regard "he" as sexist, say "he or she." If you believe your reader regards "chairperson" as a linguistic abomination, say "chairwoman" or "head of the committee." The point is that some usages are red flags that can distract attention from your content. On the other hand, when reading, you hurt yourself by being needlessly distracted or put off by language that fails to be gender neutral (or that seems *too* conscious of gender, for that matter). Despite recent attention to the issue, non-sex-specific constructions were rare before 1980, and many excellent contemporary writers still believe centuries of usage have established that the male gender can properly be used to refer either to the male or to both sexes, and they continue to use it when necessary. Some contemporary writers even argue that using female pronouns and gender-neutral construction is historically inaccurate (for example: "Each of the well-known ancient philosophers expressed his or her ideas differently") or obscures current gender inequalities ("Every president of a Fortune 500 company relies greatly on his or her staff").

I'd urge pragmatism and tolerance. Don't be puritanical about other people's attitudes, and don't assume that all writers who use "he," "him," "mankind," and so on gender neutrally are sexist or that their works are unworthy of careful study. The same goes for writers who are careful to maintain gender neutrality or use "she" neutrally. Holding past generations to contemporary standards is a common mistake.

TONE AND FORMALITY

*U*nlike the book you are now reading, college papers are normally written in a more formal style. You will want to set an objective, dispassionate tone; the last thing you need is to sound biased and unwilling to see both sides, let alone hysterical. Remember that you are trying with good arguments to persuade a reasonable person of the truth of your thesis. Use language that is appropriate to that task.

As I said in Chapter 5, it's important that you interpret what you are reading charitably. If you put the worst, most implausible interpretation on what you criticize, then you are likely to be accused of the straw man fallacy (see Chapter 4). Always assume the article or book you read was written by a well-meaning, intelligent person, not an evil-hearted fool.

The language of casual conversation is often very different from what is expected in a college paper, even when the ideas are the same. When writing for classes, find ways of expressing yourself that do not use such colloquial and informal expressions as "it really bugs me" and "this is completely crazy"—both of which I have seen in student papers.

Figures of speech have a short shelf life and, like the phrase "shelf life," quickly become either clichés or outdated. Though writing imaginatively is good, it's safest to avoid jargon unless you have a good ear for selecting colorful, useful expressions out of a sea of trite, hackneyed phrases. Here are some examples to avoid:

> you can't turn back the clock ("return to the past" is better)
>
> at this point in time (use "now")
>
> the bottom line (use "the result")
>
> a different ball game (use "a different situation")

The best rule here is to be conservative: if you think an expression may be trite or maybe not exactly the right one, you can never go wrong substituting plain language.

Besides clichés, also avoid mixed metaphors; think what such expressions *mean* before you use them. Here's an example of what not to do:

> When her game was at its peak, the crunch came.

And another:

> The argument was ironclad; its premises were watertight.

PASSIVE AND ACTIVE VOICE

n the passive voice, the subject of the sentence is acted upon; in the active voice, the subject of the sentence acts. For example:

> **Passive:** The first moment I laid eyes on her will always be cherished by me.
>
> **Active:** I will always cherish the moment I first laid eyes on her.

Sometimes, using the passive voice emphasizes the subject or brings welcome variation in sentence structure. More often, though, passive voice seems labored and weak. The active form is simpler and more forceful. The habit of using active voice also forces you to think carefully about who is doing what, to whom, and for what reason. Finally, active voice allows you to use fewer words.

Here are more examples. Note in each case how the active voice allows shorter sentences. (I could have just said: "Note in each case the writer is allowed by the active voice to write shorter sentences." But, as usual, the shorter sentence in active voice is better. Or I could have said this, which is also too long though not in the passive voice: "Notice how in each case using the active voice allows you to write shorter sentences.")

Passive: The passive voice is almost always best avoided by you.
Active: You're almost always better off using the active voice.

Passive: My first trip to England will always be remembered by me as the best.
Active: I will always remember my first trip to England as the best.

Passive: Tom was hit by a car and was killed.
Active: A car hit Tom, and he was killed.
Or: A car hit and killed Tom.

Passive: It wasn't long before he came to regret what he had done.
Active: He soon regretted his action.

COMMONLY MISSPELLED WORDS

 ere is a list of words that students often do not spell correctly. You should learn to spell them, since you will sometimes have to write without the benefit of spell-check—in written examinations, for instance.

accessible	conscientious	hypocrite
accommodate	conscious	install
aesthetic	consciousness	installment
all right	condemn	irrelevant
apparent	consensus	irresistible
arguing	deterrent	knowledgeable
argument	exaggerate	license
benefited	existence	likelihood
bulletin	fascist	maintenance
commitment	fulfill	manageable
conceive	guaranteed	naive
conscience	harass	occur

occurred

occurrence

omit

omitted

opponent

optimistic

overrule

parallel

permissible

quantitative

reference

referred

representative

responsible

seize

separate

sovereignty

subtle (adjective)

subtlety (abstract noun)

subtly (adverb)

supersede

tariff

willful

COMMONLY CONFUSED AND MISUSED WORDS

 ollowing are some of the words and phrases most commonly confused or misused by students. If you are uncertain about their meaning, look them up in a dictionary. All are good words to have in your vocabulary.

affect and effect

advise and advice

allusion and illusion

capital and capitol

choose and chose

cite, sight, and site

complement and compliment

contemptible and contemptuous

credible and credulous

criterion and criteria

dependent and dependant

deprecate and depreciate

descent and dissent

disillusion and delusion

disinterested and uninterested

eligible and illegible

eminent, imminent, and immanent

exceptional and exceptionable

hypothesis and hypotheses

imply and infer

insure and ensure

its and it's

less and fewer

loose and lose

might and may

militate and mitigate

moral and morale

persecute and prosecute

phenomenon and phenomena

precede and proceed

prescribe and proscribe

principal and principle

refute and dispute

simple and simplistic

systemic and systematic

their and there

thesis and theses

who's and whose

your and you're

grammar

INCOMPLETE SENTENCES

Always use complete sentences. That sounds obvious, but it's common to find sentence fragments—even long ones—without a subject and a main verb. Remember that a sentence expresses a complete thought or idea.

Incorrect: Hume argued that it is impossible logically to infer what ought to be from what is. Which is a question that has interested philosophy ever since. ("Which is . . . since" is not a complete sentence: what idea does it express?)

Correct: Hume argued that it is impossible logically to infer what ought to be from what is. It is a question that has interested philosophy ever since.

Incorrect: Hurrying led to confused prose and bad arguments. At a time when the country needed clarity from its leadership.

Correct: Hurrying led to confused prose and bad arguments at a time when the country needed clarity from its leadership.

Also correct: Hurrying led to confused prose and bad arguments. It was a time when the country needed clarity from its leadership.

Incorrect: Peter Singer defends the principle that if something bad will happen, we ought to prevent it unless helping will sacrifice something of comparable moral importance. Which leads him to conclude most of us should provide aid to the hungry.

Correct: Peter Singer defends the principle that if something bad will happen, we ought to prevent it unless helping will sacrifice something of comparable moral importance. He concludes from this that most of us should provide aid to the hungry.

RUN-ON AND FUSED SENTENCES

 run-on sentence is one in which too many dependent clauses are run together into a single sentence. Correct it by breaking the sentence up, eliminating the conjunctions that join the clauses.

Incorrect: I will argue that the issue has been misunderstood by almost everybody, and then after making a relevant distinction show why the topic is not nearly as difficult as is usually thought.

Correct: I will argue that the issue has been misunderstood by almost everybody. After making a relevant distinction, I will show why the topic is not nearly as difficult as is usually thought.

Another mistake is a *fused sentence*. This means joining two independent clauses, which could serve as complete sentences, without the necessary punctuation or connecting words.

Incorrect: Thomson's article is excellent she uses a very clever analogy.

Also incorrect: Thomson's article is excellent, she uses a very clever analogy.

Correct: Thomson's article is excellent; she uses a very clever analogy.

Also correct: Thomson's article is excellent. In it, she uses a very clever analogy.

PRONOUN AGREEMENT

 ere are some examples of failure of agreement between a pronoun and its antecedent:

Incorrect: None of us are perfect.

Correct: None of us is perfect. (Remember: none = no *one*.)

Incorrect: Legislators may defer its ruling.

Correct: Legislators may defer their ruling.

Also correct: The legislature may defer its ruling.

Incorrect: The group of people felt they had . . .

Correct: The group of people felt it had . . .

Incorrect: The South objected. They argued . . .

Correct: Southerners objected. They argued . . .

Incorrect: Many people who study mathematics find if you can't follow it the first time you should read it again.

Correct: Many people who study mathematics find that if they can't follow it the first time, they should read it again.

Also correct: Often one who studies mathematics finds that it is impossible to follow the first time and must be read again.

Here's another example—one that's especially troubling as well as quite common:

Incorrect: When someone takes that position, they are giving up their rights. (*Someone* is singular; *they* is plural.)

Correct: When people take that position, they are giving up their rights.

This comes up because, when faced with the gendered pronoun issues discussed earlier, many writers throw up their hands. In this case, the first example uses the plural "they" as a substitute for the singular but awkward "his or her." I suggest you try to avoid all three errors: using the gender-neutral "he" or "him," using pronouns that disagree, and using the cumbersome "he or she." That may require some ingenuity on your part. If you can't find a way out and must choose which error to make, all I can say is, "You're on your own. Good luck."

PRONOUN CASE

 emember that subjects require the subjective or nominative case (for example, I, he, she, they, we, or who), while objects of a verb or preposition require the objective case (me, him, her, them, us, or whom).

Incorrect: Johnson is a better player than her.

Correct: Johnson is a better player than she. (Try completing the sentence as a test: "a better player than she is.")

Incorrect: The professor criticized her and I.

Correct: The professor criticized her and me. (i.e., criticized me)

Incorrect: Sue writes better than me.

Correct: Sue writes better than I. (i.e., than I write)

You should never use "me" as a subject. The nominative pronoun "I" is correct and follows other subjects in the sentence.

Incorrect: Me and Eric think Shakespeare is fascinating.

Correct: Eric and I think Shakespeare is fascinating.

You would never say, "Me thinks Shakespeare is fascinating," so don't say "X and me" either, let alone "Me and X."

MISPLACED PRONOUNS

 isplaced pronouns can cause considerable confusion. Be sure the referent of every pronoun is clear.

Incorrect: Farmers hated ranchers because of their prejudice. (Who was prejudiced—farmers or ranchers?)

Correct: Farmers, because of their prejudice, hated ranchers.

Also correct: Farmers hated ranchers because ranchers were prejudiced.

Note how this example nicely illustrates a point I have often made: that paying attention to writing helps or even forces clarity of thinking.

SUBJECT/VERB AGREEMENT

 ubject and verb must agree in number (singular or plural). When they don't, one cause is confusion about the number of the subject. Here is an example where "neither/nor" is mistakenly treated as plural.

Incorrect: Neither Plato nor Aristotle were as great as many people suppose.

Correct: Neither Plato nor Aristotle was as great as many people suppose.

When a subject and a verb are separated in a sentence, their failure to agree in number can go unnoticed. This is especially true when the subject of the sentence is not obvious.

Incorrect: The difficulty of the issues presented in the articles frustrate many students.

Correct: The difficulty of the issues presented in the articles frustrates many students.

Incorrect: A large number of ideas were discussed.

Correct: A large number of ideas was discussed.

Also correct: Many ideas were discussed.

To check for this mistake, use the familiar test of putting the subject and the verb together. In these examples, you would not say "Ideas was discussed . . ." or "The difficulty frustrate . . ."

Finally, if you have two subjects, one singular and the other plural, the verb should match the subject nearest to it.

Incorrect: Neither Hume nor modern empiricists concludes that morality is useless—only that it isn't scientific.

Correct: Neither Hume nor modern empiricists conclude that morality is useless—only that it isn't scientific.

Again, ask yourself whether you'd say "modern empiricists concludes. . . ."

FAULTY PARALLELISM

 e sure that all the words, phrases, and sentences you write in a series have a parallel structure. Here are some common examples of faulty parallelism.

Incorrect: The result of arguing that way is to appear inconsistent.

Correct: The result of arguing that way is appearing inconsistent.

Incorrect: In this paper, I hope to accomplish the following: criticize the position taken by Brandt, demonstrate how Brandt might answer my objection, and responding to his answer.

Correct: In this paper, I hope to accomplish the following: criticize the position taken by Brandt, demonstrate how he might answer my objection, and respond to his answer.

SPLIT INFINITIVES

ome people regard a split infinitive as a serious grammatical sin, but others are more relaxed about it as long as it does not sound too awkward. To be sure, I'd avoid it.

Incorrect: To quickly run
Correct: To run quickly
Also correct: Quickly to run

Incorrect: To inaccurately say
Correct: To say inaccurately
Also correct: Inaccurately to say

Incorrect: A word processor allows you to repeatedly revise a text.
Correct: A word processor allows you to revise a text repeatedly.

punctuation

APOSTROPHES

Apostrophes serve two purposes: they indicate omission and possession. *Omission* shows where letters have been omitted in contractions; *possession* indicates that a noun possesses its object.

Examples of omission include: *didn't, aren't, isn't, they're,* and *who's* (abbreviation for "who is"). Typically the apostrophe marks the place where letters are missing: for example, *should not* becomes *shouldn't; she will* becomes *she'll; he had* becomes *he'd.*

Examples of the use of an apostrophe to indicate possession are given below. The basic rule is that words that do not end in the letter *s* form the possessive by adding '*s*, while words ending in *s* as well as plural nouns ending in *s* add an apostrophe after the final letter.

> a genius' work (the work of a genius)
>
> the student's class (the class of one student)
>
> the students' class (the class of more than one student)
>
> the students' classes (the classes of more than one student)

One exception to this rule is proper nouns:

> Rawls's book or Rawls' book
>
> Charles' sister or Charles's sister
>
> J. S. Mill's argument
>
> C. Wright Mills' or Mills's argument (the author's name is Mills, not Mill)

Don't use an apostrophe in possessive pronouns: *yours, hers, ours, theirs,* or *its* (when it means belonging to it). The exception to this is *one* and its derivatives (for example, *someone's paper, somebody else's paper*).

Be careful about words that sound alike but are spelled differently and have different meanings. For example *whose* (possessive, as in "Whose knife is this?") and *who's* (contraction of *who* and *is,* as in "Who's going to the store with me?").

Don't confuse *it's* with *its. It's* is an abbreviation of *it is* (or *it has*), while *its* is a possessive pronoun. For example:

> I chased the dog, but it's difficult to know where it's gone looking for its bone.

Note that *the 1960's* is incorrect, unless you mean it to be possessive. For instance:

> The 1960's greatest hits were not that great.

Otherwise, it should be *the 1960s.* For example:

> He slept through the 1960s.

Finally, here are some examples of how these rules are combined:

> the boy's parent's car (one parent, one boy)
>
> the boys' parent's care (one parent, more than one boy)
>
> the boy's parents' car (two parents, one boy)
>
> the boys' parents' car (two or more parents and two or more boys)

COLONS

One use of a colon is to indicate the start of a list or a long quotation.

> He brought many items along: a watch, a bookmark, a hiking compass, and a piece of candy.

> Jefferson wrote the "Declaration of Independence," in which he said the following: "We hold these truths to be self-evident, that . . ."

Colons can also be used to explain, summarize, or illustrate what has just been said.

> One thing is certain: students will continue to make mistakes with punctuation.

> After much soul-searching, he finally decided: he would tell the dean.

As this last example nicely illustrates, a colon can add strength or emphasis to a sentence.

COMMAS

The comma is generally used to indicate a pause within a sentence. If in doubt about a sentence, read it aloud and notice when you pause slightly. Here are some problems caused by the absence or wrong placing of the comma:

> **Incorrect:** The Republicans who had nominated Eisenhower in 1952, won the election.

> **Incorrect:** The Republicans, who had nominated Eisenhower in 1952 won the election.

> **Correct:** The Republicans, who had nominated Eisenhower in 1952, won the election.

Avoid adding unnecessary commas. For example:

> **Incorrect:** The lack of good leadership, did nothing to help matters.

> **Correct:** The lack of good leadership did nothing to help matters.

Don't use the comma to link together separate sentences, thereby creating a run-on sentence.

> **Incorrect:** This advice is sensible, we hope that you will follow it.

> **Correct:** This advice is sensible. We hope that you will follow it.

Also correct: This advice is sensible; we hope that you will follow it.

Also correct: This advice is sensible, and we hope that you will follow it. (Note here that without the "and," it would be a run-on sentence, so you would need to use a semicolon instead of the comma plus "and.")

Incorrect: This advice is sensible, however many of you will ignore it.

Correct: This advice is sensible. However, many of you will ignore it.

Also correct: This advice is sensible; however, many of you will ignore it.

The misuse of commas in relative clauses can cause inadvertent changes of meaning. Compare:

Scientists who accept Darwin condemned the new book.

Scientists, who accept Darwin, condemned the new book.

Obviously, these two sentences do not mean the same thing. If you are doubtful, read the two sentences aloud (as I always recommend). The second implies that *all* scientists accept Darwin, while the first says that only those scientists who accept Darwin also condemn the new book.

Using commas correctly is one of the biggest challenges students face. But you are not alone. Oscar Wilde supposedly once said that "I have spent most of the day putting in a comma and the rest of the day taking it out." It may be helpful, therefore, if I list some of the basic rules for using commas.

1. Use commas to *separate the items you are listing in a series.* Thus, you should say:

   She has written good books on Mill, Darwin, and Marx.

2. Use a comma to *separate the introductory phrase of a sentence.* Here is an example:

   Hoping to do well on the exam, she studied her notes carefully.

3. Use a comma *before a short conjunction that connects two independent clauses* of a sentence. Short conjunctions are *so, for, but, and,* and *yet.* So, for example, you should punctuate this way:

   The girl did not think she was good in math, so she was surprised she got the best grade.

4. Use a comma to *set off a part of the sentence that is not essential* and thus can be removed without changing the sentence's basic meaning. For instance:

   Anybody who goes along with him, for whatever reason, will be in trouble with the sheriff.

5. Use commas to *set off parenthetical remarks* (such as "however") or *interjections* (such as commands and expressions of emotion). Here are examples of each:

> It is always best, of course, to take the time to prepare at least a first draft.

> She is right, as I argued in the last section, to conclude that happiness is not always valuable.

> Yes, you were definitely right.

6. Use commas *to separate adjectives,* but only when you could substitute an "and" in the sentence. So, for instance, you might write:

> She is a brilliant, thoughtful writer. ("She is a brilliant and thoughtful writer" also makes sense.)

But compare that with:

> It was a bright green color. (You would not say "bright and green," so you don't need a comma.)

7. Use commas to *separate the parts of a quotation.*

> "The problem with the argument," he wrote, "is that it ignores the following possibility."

An important exception to this rule is when the quoted material follows the word "that."

> She concluded with the observation that "This book's major strength is its originality."

SEMICOLONS

*t*he semicolon can be used to separate independent clauses that could have been two (or occasionally more) separate but very closely related sentences. With a semicolon, they become a single sentence. (See the examples above as well.)

> The question is provided by the author; the conclusion comes from the readers.

Semicolons can also be used in a series in which the items already have commas.

Included in the invitation list were his wife; their daughter, Helen; the monk who went to Tibet; and many of Helen's friends, some of whom were also her partners.

CAPITALIZATION

*C*apitalize *proper nouns,* that is, the names of specific people, places, or things. These include religions (Islam); the days of the week, holidays, and months (Monday, Christmas, November); basic geographical divisions (Arctic Circle, the Northeast); rivers, lakes, and mountains (Rocky Mountains, Lake Woebegone); historical periods and documents (Middle Ages, the U.S. Constitution); political parties and entities (Democratic Party); legislative and judicial bodies (Supreme Court, Parliament, Congress); treaties and laws (the Versailles Treaty, the Voting Rights Act); and nations, streets, cities and towns, and languages (Germany, Main Street, Denver, English).

Do not capitalize the first letter of the first word of a sentence following a colon.

He left no doubt at all: this was to be a great moment.

QUOTATION MARKS AND SCARE QUOTES

*t*he basic rule is to use quotation marks when you quote directly and the quotation is no more than four lines long. If the quotation is more than four lines, indent it and don't use quotation marks. Also use quotation marks for titles of short works, such as essays, poems, and articles (you should italicize titles of books).

Quotation marks can also be used when you want to mention a word rather than actually use it in a sentence. For example:

The term "justice" has many meanings.

Another option is to use single quotation marks as *scare quotes* to indicate irony or that you don't mean what is said literally. For instance:

The war was over, and 'justice' was achieved.

It's easy to overuse quotation marks and scare quotes. Never use them when you don't have a specific reason.

PLACEMENT OF PUNCTUATION

lways put commas and periods *inside* quotation marks, and put colons and semicolons *outside* quotation marks.

"You cannot hope to succeed," she said, "unless you focus on your writing."

In her lecture on the modern novel, Professor James warned against "reification"; I'm not sure I understood what she meant.

I've noticed many college topics that are coming to be termed "practical": abortion, affirmative action, and capital punishment, to name only a few.

Question marks and exclamation marks go inside or outside other quotations depending on sense. If the punctuation is part of the quotation, it belongs inside the quotation mark.

"When will the American Medical Association finally take a position on affirmative action?" asked the speaker.

He asked "Why?"

Why did he say "Why"?

SOME ADDITIONAL RULES

ere are some other basic rules involving punctuation and the general layout of the paper.

1. Short quotations (that is, less than about 50 words) should be enclosed in double quotation marks and run in with the main text. Use single quotation marks for quotations within quotations: "We have learned that 'more is not necessarily better.'" Longer quotations should be separated from the main text by being indented without quotation marks.

2. Interpolations within quotations are permissible if enclosed in square brackets (never parenthesis). For example: "To be true to ourselves [he argued] we must be true to others."

3. Ellipses within a quoted sentence should be indicated by three spaced periods. Be sure to leave a space before the first period. Ellipses at the end of a sentence should be indicated by three spaced periods and the sentence period, that is, four periods in all.

APPENDIX I

additional
resources

OTHER WORKS ON WRITING AND STUDYING

You have a wide choice of books to get more help improving your writing skills. Some emphasize writing, grammar, and punctuation in general; others focus more specifically on writing papers. On the following page are a few I recommend. If they are not in your library, almost any bookstore can order them.

The Chicago Manual of Style. 14th ed. Chicago: University of Chicago Press, 1993.

Hodges, John C., et. al. *Harbrace College Handbook.* 13th ed. Fort Worth: Harcourt Brace, 1998.

Gibaldi, Joseph. *MLA. Handbook for Writers of Research Papers.* 6th ed. New York: Modern Language Association of America, 2003.

Strunk, William J., and E. B. White. *Elements of Style.* 4th ed. Boston: Allyn and Bacon, 1999.

Turabian, Kate L. *Student's Guide for Writing College Papers.* 6th ed. Chicago: University of Chicago Press, 1996.

The Vest-Pocket Writer's Guide. Boston: Houghton Mifflin, 1987.

You can also access Strunk and White's *Elements of Style* on the Internet. It's a valuable resource on most aspects of writing. The URL is <www.bartleby.com/141>.

A PAPER ASSESSMENT FORM

Author of essay under review:

Name of reviewer:

Instructions to Students

Here are some guidelines that will help you in evaluating your own work or the work of others. Answer each question, but also feel free to make any additional comments you think will be helpful. After you have received the assessment of your own paper, consider each of the responses carefully. If the reviewer had problems understanding part of your paper, try reading what you wrote aloud and asking yourself if you think it is clear. If not, then you have probably not yet developed the ideas well enough in your own mind, or perhaps they just weren't expressed well. Consider other writing problems in the same way, asking yourself why the reviewer was confused or objected to something. Think about all the objections that have been raised. Do they have merit? How can you fix them? Then rewrite your paper from scratch, thinking not only about how to correct the problems already identified in the review but also about how you can make other improvements. Rewriting is a critical step; it is here that you will make the most progress. Always remember: the key to good writing is editing. No paper is ever so good that it cannot be improved by further editing and rewriting.

Assessment Questions

1. What are the strengths of this essay?

2. Do the title and introductory paragraph give a clear sense of the subject as well as of the author's approach and general conclusion? If not, would clarifying these improve the paper?

3. Is the paper's organizational structure reasonably clear? If not, how could it be improved?

4. Is some of the paper's wording unclear, making it difficult to figure out what the author is saying? If so, indicate which sentences are unclear and, if possible, how they might be improved.

5. Does the paper have problems with language? Look carefully at the discussions in this book of verbosity, bloated language, pronoun and verb tenses, gendered pronouns, tone and formality, and passive and active voice. Do writing errors detract from the paper? If so, underline them and explain why in the margin.

6. Does the paper have errors in spelling or word usage? If so, underline them and indicate how you think the wording problems could be fixed.

7. Does the paper have grammar or punctuation errors? Review the relevant chapters in this book for help. If you find problems, indicate where they are in the paper and how you think they can be corrected.

8. Do you think the author has understood the authors discussed in the paper? If not, where does the paper's author go wrong in interpretation?

9. Does the paper have too much summary of other people's positions and not enough of the author's ideas? Or vice versa? Explain.

10. Are there specific places where you think the author's argument or position needs to be better substantiated? Has the author provided evidence for the conclusions or merely offered personal opinion?

11. Does the author make questionable assumptions that need to be supported? If so, explain.

12. Does the author fail to address possible problems or objections to the argument? If so, explain the objections you think needed discussing.

13. Describe how this paper might be improved. What advice would you give the author as he revises it for presentation to the instructor? Be as specific as you can.

Keep in mind that its not unusual for people to be a bit upset after being criticized about their writing. Maybe because writing is so personal, so close to speech, criticism of it can easily feel like criticism of you. Yet one of the best things you can learn in college is to regard writing as a craft or skill and your essays as products you are trying to perfect. If you were trying to improve your tennis game or your cooking skills, you'd want the opinions of others. Writing is no different; everybody benefits from constructive criticism. In fact, we're all lucky if we have it available. For example, I have gotten some very helpful criticism of this book from my wife, Amy, who used to be a newspaper columnist. Indeed, she suggested I add this last paragraph (though not the previous sentence)!

I have used this form in my classes in three different ways: by asking students to use it in their own writing and rewriting; by having a fellow student use it, who thereby earns the honored title of "peer reviewer"; and by using it myself as a guide in commenting on students' work. Having students answer these questions about their own papers forces them to look closely at the different ways a paper is judged, much like another person would. Sometimes I ask students to exchange papers, to use this form as a guide for making comments on each others' papers, and then to rewrite their own paper in light of the reviewer's comments. I then have them turn in both their original draft, with comments, and their final paper. This *peer review* process encourages discussions among students and helps to improve the writing of both the reviewer and the writer.

COPY-EDITING SYMBOLS

i find it helpful in commenting on papers to use abbreviations and symbols. It saves lots of time, but to work effectively there must be a convention about what such symbols mean. Here are the ones I've found most helpful. Your professors may use them, or you may use them yourself as you do peer evaluation or review your own papers.

SYMBOL	CHANGE NEEDED
is at (at)	omit item (word, punctuation, sentence, or paragraph) inside circle
in to	close; no space needed
to boldly state	transpose words or letters
want go (to)	insert this word (or these words) here
#	add a space
w	capitalize
W	lowercase letter
¶	create a paragraph
P	punctuation error
SP	spelling error
IS	incomplete sentence; sentence fragment
AG	agreement error
RS	run-on sentence
FS	fused sentence
PAR	parallelism error
WOR	wordy sentence; should be shortened
WC	poor word choice
REP	repetitive use of a word or phrase
U	unclear meaning; sentence or word is vague or imprecise
FN	footnote needed

answers

FOR CHAPTER 4: LOGIC AND CRITICAL THINKING

1. We test our ideas, theories, and so on by debating and arguing. Reasoning is the method we use to discover the merit of those ideas and theories; it involves giving arguments rather than, for instance, threatening people and using force. Reasoning concerns not what in fact persuades people, but what should persuade them—that is, what they have good evidence for accepting.

2. A. Statements are uses of language in which we say something that is either true or false, as opposed to other times when we may use language to ask a question, express a feeling, or utter a warning.

   B. Arguments are two or more statements with a certain form: at least one premise and one conclusion.

   C. Premises are statements that are supposed to provide good reasons for accepting another statement, namely, the conclusion.

3. Inductive arguments are ones in which if the premises are true, then the conclusion is probably or most likely true. Inductive arguments do not provide conclusive grounds for accepting the conclusion. Deductive arguments are ones in which the premises, if true, do establish the conclusion with certainty; if the premises of a deductive argument are true, the conclusion must be true. The four types of inductive arguments identified in the text are generalizations, predictions, causal inferences, and analogies.

4. Have the students bring their editorials to class and read some of them. Then have the students explain why they thought an argument was presented and what it was, followed by a general discussion of whether or not other students agree.

5. Have students bring their notebooks to class and discuss their examples with the other students.

6. The form of a statement does not depend on its specific meaning or categories. So, for example, "All horses are mammals" and "All sunsets are wondrous" have the same form.

7. All animals are alive; no dogs are cats; some people are mean; some trees are dead.

8. All A is B (or All As are Bs).

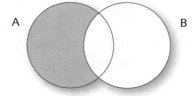

No A is B.

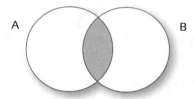

Some A is B.

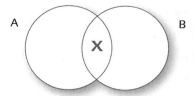

Some A is not B.

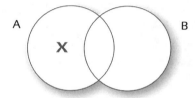

9. Contradictories have opposite truth values—that is, if one is true, the other must be false, and vice versa. "All A is B" and "Some A is not B" are contradictories, as are "No A is B" and "Some A is B." Contraries cannot both be true. "All A is B" and "No A is B" are contraries. Subcontraries cannot both be false. "Some A is B" and "Some A is not B" are subcontraries. "Subaltern" refers to the relationship between the universal and its corresponding particular, whether positive or negative. So if the universal affirmative "All A is B" is true, then the corresponding particular affirmative "Some A is B" is true, while if "Some A is B" is false, then "All A is B" is false. Similarly, if the universal negative "No A is B" is true, then its subaltern, "Some A is not B," is also true, and if "Some A is not B" is false, then "No A is B" is also false.

10. The converse of a statement is one in which the subject and the predicate are reversed. So "No A is B" has as its converse "No B is A." The converse is equivalent for both the E form ("No A is B") and the I form ("Some A is B").

11. Obversion occurs by changing from negative to positive or from positive to negative and replacing the second or predicate class with its complement. So, for instance, "Some A is B" has as its obverse "Some A is not non-B." The obverse is equivalent for all four of the categorical propositions.

12. Contraposition is like conversion, except that in addition to switching the subject and predicate classes, each is replaced with its complement. So "All A is B" has as its contrapositive "All non-B is non-A." It is equivalent for the universal affirmative A form and the particular negative O form—that is, for "All A is B" and "Some A is not B."

13. A. All women are emotionally stronger than men.

     B. No firefighters are cowards, or All firefighters are noncowards.

     C. All persons who buy a ticket are people who win a prize.

     D. All things that are illegal are things done by criminals, or All actions that are illegal are actions done by criminals.

     E. No person who goes to that store is a person who should have a clear conscience, or All persons who go to that store are people who should not have a clear conscience.

     F. Some people who speak are people who speak out of turn.

     G. All lovers are friends.

     H. Some friends are not lovers.

     I. All persons who are reading this are literate persons.

     J. All persons who still support Communism are fools.

     K. All capitalists are exploiters.

     L. All persons who have met both Tom and Tim are persons who prefer Tom.

     M. All D (where D is the class with the one member, Dracula) are things that love to eat out.

     N. All T (where T is the class made up of Tom) is a person who is neither mean nor angry, or No T is a person who is either mean or angry.

     O. All things that exist are things that are made of matter.

     P. All times I go to the beach are times it does not rain, or No times I go to the beach are times it rains.

Q. All cats that are smart are tigers, or No cats that are smart are nontigers.

R. All people who should be on the field are winners, or No persons who should be on the field are nonwinners.

S. All students who did not fail the exam are students who can leave, AND No students who failed the exam are students who can leave. (This requires two categorical statements.)

14. A. All Ps are Ds and All Ds are Ms; therefore, All Ps are Ms.

    B. Some Cs are As, so some As are Cs.

    C. No Ws are Cs and All Ps are Ws; therefore, No Ps are Cs.

    D. All H is B and No M is H; therefore, No M is B.

15. A.

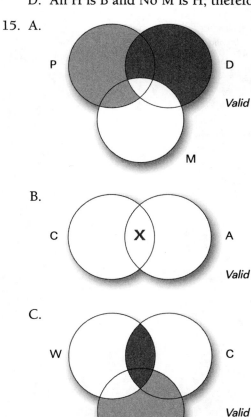

B.

C.

D.

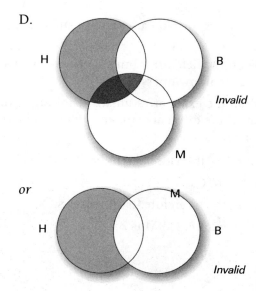

or

16. Answers will vary.

a poem
about rules

On the following page is a poem by a former student of mine, Anna Feigenbaum.[1] She wrote it in response to my having asked her and others in my class to use this book.

---

[1] © 2002 Anna Feigenbaum. Anna kindly gave me her permission to reprint it here.

GRAMMAR AND OTHER DISEASES, AFTER JOHN ARTHUR'S *A CONCISE GUIDE TO COLLEGE SUCCESS*

It all started last month
when I put a staple
in the bottom right hand corner.
For the third week in a row
I had forgotten my page numbers.
And now, my language is bloated.
Not to mention,
I'm suffering from problems of the gendered pronoun.
I swore to myself it was the last time
I'd misplace those pronouns.
I've searched everywhere
but I think they're just gone.
Plus, the medication they've given
for my parallelism
has caused a splitting infinitive between my temples.

My friends,
You'd think they'd be here in this time of need, but
Verb and I never seem to agree anymore.
(He says I am way too passive.)
And I've fused so many sentences
that Semi-colon won't talk to me;
She thinks I have a fear of independence.
And yesterday, as if things could get any worse,
I scared the Quotes.
Ironically, they took me too literally when I said,
"So long as there is 'grammar' there is God!"[2]

---

[2]A posthumous thank you to Neitzsche for this quotation.

index